# Sports and Courts

# Sports and Courts

An Introduction to Principles of
Law and Legal Theory Using Cases
from Professional Sports

*Frederick J. Day*

iUniverse, Inc.
New York  Lincoln  Shanghai

# Sports and Courts
## An Introduction to Principles of Law and Legal Theory Using Cases from Professional Sports

iUniverse books may be ordered through booksellers or by contacting:

iUniverse
2021 Pine Lake Road, Suite 100
Lincoln, NE 68512
www.iuniverse.com
1-800-Authors (1-800-288-4677)

ISBN: 0-595-34315-5

Printed in the United States of America

# Contents

# Introduction:
# A Modern-Day *Palsgraf*

Plaintiff was standing on a platform of defendant's railroad after buying a ticket to go to Rockaway Beach. A train stopped at the station, bound for another place. Two men ran forward to catch it. One of the men reached the platform of the car without mishap, though the train was already moving. The other man, carrying a package, jumped aboard the car, but seemed unsteady as if about to fall. A guard on the car, who had held the door open, reached forward to help him in, and another guard on the platform pushed him from behind. In this act, the package was dislodged, and fell upon the rails. It was a package of small size, about fifteen inches long, and was covered by a newspaper. In fact it contained fireworks, but there was nothing in its appearance to give notice of its contents. The fireworks when they fell exploded. The shock of the explosion threw down some scales at the other end of the platform many feet away. The scales struck the plaintiff, causing injuries for which she sues.

—Justice Benjamin Cardozo's description of the
underlying facts in the case of *Palsgraf v. Long Island R. R. Co.*,
248 N.Y. 339, 162 N.E. 99 (1928).

Early in the morning of May 18, 2000, the New York Knicks basketball team returned home from a game in Miami. As the team's plane taxied to the spot where the Knicks had parked their vehicles, one of the plane's engines emitted an extraordinary amount of thrust. It was a freak blast. The concussion picked up the 1995 Honda Civic owned by Knicks head coach Jeff Van Gundy and tossed it "like a tumbleweed" on top of several other cars.[1]

---

[1] Mike Wise, "From Team to Car, Woe Is Van Gundy," *The N.Y. Times*, 29 May 2000, D3.

Van Gundy emerged from the incident as a rather curious fellow. There is something quixotic about a head coach at the highest level of professional sports who drives a five-year-old Honda Civic. Seventy years earlier, the tardy railroad passenger emerged, similarly, as a curious figure in the case of *Palsgraf v. Long Island Railroad Co.* What was the gentleman doing carrying a load of fireworks, concealed by a covering of newspapers, onto the Long Island Railroad train? From light-weight Honda Civics, concealed fireworks, and curious fellows, the law produces compelling **tort** cases.

The similarities between the *Palsgraf* case and the Van Gundy incident are striking. *Palsgraf* involved a train; the Van Gundy incident an airplane. In *Palsgraf*, the explosion came from fireworks that were under wrap; in Van Gundy, from a freak blast out of the plane's engine. In *Palsgraf*, the explosion sent some railroad scales flying; in Van Gundy, the blast sent the coach's Honda Civic flying.

Justice Cardozo isn't around to help sort out liability in the Van Gundy case. Fortunately, though, he left behind his decision in *Palsgraf*. From *Palsgraf*, we learn that where a **plaintiff** alleges **negligent conduct**, the law must find "a risk to another or to others within the **range of apprehension**."

For a sports fan, it is the setting that distinguishes the Van Gundy matter from *Palsgraf*. The Van Gundy incident arose in the context of sports. It is the story of a coach who had just suffered a demoralizing loss in a playoff game and then returned home to find his car demolished. It is a story that would find its way onto the sports pages and into *Sports Illustrated*.

Why write a book that focuses exclusively on cases from the world of sports? Just as there are people who turn first to the sports pages each morning, there are students of the law and others who are drawn to sports cases. Invariably, for a sports fan, it is more exhilarating, if not easier, to learn the law when the lessons are presented in the context of sports. A primary purpose of this book, then, is to provide a tool in the learning process for sports fans who are studying the law.

There is another purpose, however, one arising out of my experiences after the publication of my first book on sports and the law, *Clubhouse Lawyer: The Sports Fan's Guide to Life and the Law*. When the book was released in November 2002, it received what might euphemistically be termed a "modest" amount of acclaim. In truth, for the better part of eight months, the book languished, in a figurative sense, well below the "**Mendoza Line**." In June 2003, however, Chicago Cubs slugger Sammy Sosa came to the rescue. In a game against the Tampa Bay Devil Rays, Sosa shattered his bat, exposing pieces of cork. Overnight, talk radio shows were abuzz with discussions of the legal and moral implications of Sosa's corked bat.

Throughout June and into July, hosts of sports-talk radio programs continually asked that I appear on the air to discuss matters such as Sosa's contention that the corked bat was a "batting practice bat" that he had used accidentally and innocently. On radio stations across the country, I was asked to weigh in on whether the punishment imposed on Sosa—suspension for seven games—was warranted, and whether the affair should, or would, affect Sosa's chances for the Hall of Fame. Before the furor died down, I had appeared as a guest on more than forty radio shows. If talk show hosts were not conversant with concepts such as premeditation and plausible denial before the bat corking incident, they certainly were afterwards.

A month after the bat corking incident, Pittsburgh Pirates first baseman Randall Simon also engaged in mischief with a baseball bat. Again, sports radio hosts were quick to pick up on the legal implications. Was Simon's act of striking 19-year-old Mandy Block, who was wearing the top-heavy costume of an Italian sausage mascot, an **assault**? Was it a **battery**? Was Simon liable for injuries suffered by the hot dog mascot, who was running next to the Italian sausage, even though he did not hit the hot dog? Would either the Italian sausage mascot or the hot dog mascot sue Simon and, if so, with what result? Would Simon be "grilled" in court? The Italian sausage episode offered another bountiful opportunity for on-the-air discussions of legal principles in the context of baseball.

The Sosa/Simon incidents demonstrated that there was a market for a fan-friendly book on sports and the law. These incidents, along with the courtroom drama over ownership of Barry Bonds' 73rd home run ball, provided the impetus for a revision of *Clubhouse Lawyer: The Sports Fan's Guide to Life and the Law.* In June 2004, the revised edition was released under the title *Clubhouse Lawyer: Law in the World of Sports.*

The Sosa and Simon stories did more than merely provide grist for another book on sports and the law. These incidents also showed there was a need for a shorthand guide to the law that sports-talk show hosts and other commentators could quickly access to gain a sense of the law as it applies in the unique environment of ballparks, football stadiums, and basketball arenas.

In *Sports and Courts*, I have tried to set down the most fascinating legal cases that the world of sports has to offer. The book is directed, in part, at students of the law. But it is also directed at radio commentators and sports fans who are undertaking the effort to learn the law—for those individuals who can appreciate the fact that Jeff Van Gundy was more upset by his team's loss to Miami than by the loss of his Honda.[2]

To readers, I hope that you will find amusement as well as enlightenment in the pages that follow.

To my colleague and friend Melissa Keefer, I express my appreciation for her diligent efforts in helping to prepare *Sports and Courts* for publication.

Fred Day
Falls Church, Virginia

---

[2] "If we had won," Van Gundy said later, "I'd have been happy to walk back from Miami."

# **Approach** Used in This Book

In 1988, Pam Postema, a professional baseball umpire assigned to the Triple-A Alliance of Professional Baseball Clubs, umpired a spring training game involving the Pittsburgh Pirates. Upon meeting Postema on the field, Chuck Tanner, the Pirates manager, asked her if she would like a kiss. To Postema, the question was offensive; to Tanner, it was simply playful.

In sports, as in so many other areas of life, situations arise that call for the administration of justice. Before justice can be administered, however, there must be a determination as to whether a wrong was committed and, if so, by which party and against which party. In the game involving Postema and the Pirates, the facts would show that Tanner never kissed the umpire. He merely asked her if she wanted a kiss.

Was Tanner's question more than an inept attempt at humor or an ill-conceived form of hazing? Did the question constitute a **tort**? Relying on the long established principle of "boys will be boys," Tanner would take the position that he did not commit a tort.

The law assumes a certain predictability and consistency. If Tanner's question constituted a tort under the law applied at the Pirates' spring training home in Bradenton, Florida, the same question, posed under the same circumstances, should constitute a tort in Pittsburgh, Pennsylvania. Conversely, if the question did not amount to a tort in Bradenton, it should not be a tort in Pittsburgh.

The Restatements of Law published by the American Law Institute form one of the primary tools available in the legal field for establishing consistency in judicial decisions—in effect for ensuring that if the threat of a kiss does not amount to a tort in Bradenton, it likewise does not constitute a tort in Pittsburgh.

*Sports and Courts* is an effort to examine principles of law in general and the Restatements in particular. The book presents a series of situations from the world of sports, each of which carries distinct legal implications. After discussing each situation, *Sports and Courts* presents an analysis that incorporates pertinent principles from the **Second Restatement of Torts** and/or the **Second Restatement of Contracts**. The analyses are in the form of summary discussions and are not intended to be a comprehensive examination of all aspects of the legal issues underlying each case.

The hope is that readers will (1) come away with a heightened appreciation of the value of the Restatements as tools for understanding and resolving legal issues and (2) derive some fun in the process.

For purposes of brevity and avoiding repetition, the discussions in this book use "Restatement of Torts" as a shorthand reference to the Second Restatement of Torts and "Restatement of Contracts" as a shorthand reference to the Second Restatement of Contracts. It should be understood that all references to the Restatements, whether of Torts or Contracts, are to the Restatements Second.

# Acknowledgments

Sections from Volumes 1 and 2 of the Restatement (Second) of Torts (1965): Copyright 1965 by the American Law Institute. All rights reserved. Reprinted with permission.

Sections from Volume 3 of the Restatement (Second) of Torts (1977): Copyright 1977 by the American Law Institute. All rights reserved. Reprinted with permission.

Sections from Volume 4 of the Restatement (Second) of Torts (1979): Copyright 1979 by the American Law Institute. All rights reserved. Reprinted with permission.

Sections from the Restatement (Second) of Contracts (1981): Copyright 1981 by the American Law Institute. All rights reserved. Reprinted with permission.

Source for Major League Baseball statistical information and data on player transactions: www.baseball-reference.com.

# A Note About the American Law Institute and the Restatements of Law

The American Law Institute was organized in 1923 following a study conducted by a group of prominent American judges, lawyers, and teachers known as "The Committee on the Establishment of a Permanent Organization for the Improvement of the Law." The Committee had reported that the two chief defects in American law, its uncertainty and its complexity, had produced a general dissatisfaction with the administration of justice.

Part of the uncertainty of the law, as it then existed, was due to the lack of agreement among members of the profession on the fundamental principles of the **common law**. Other causes of uncertainty included the lack of precision in the use of legal terms, conflicting and badly drawn statutory provisions, a nearly uncontrollable volume of recorded decisions, and the number and nature of novel legal questions.

The Committee on the Establishment of a Permanent Organization for the Improvement of the Law recommended that an organization be formed to improve the law and its administration. In short order, the American Law Institute was established. The purposes of the Institute were to: (1) promote the clarification and simplification of the law; (2) make the law more readily adaptable to social needs; and (3) secure better administration of justice.

The Committee recommended that the first undertaking of the Institute should be directed at addressing uncertainty in the law through a restatement of basic legal subjects. The Committee anticipated that the restatement would serve as a mechanism for advising judges and lawyers regarding principles of common law. The formulation of such a restatement thus became the first endeavor of the Institute. Between 1923 and 1944, Restatements of the Law were developed in the areas of the Law of Agency, Conflict of Laws, Contracts, Judgments, Property, Restitution, Security, Torts, and Trusts.

In 1952, the Institute began work on the second series of Restatements—new editions of the original Restatements that updated them, reflected new analyses and concepts, and expanded upon the authorities used in reaching the conclusions set forth. The Institute released Volumes 1 and 2 of the Second Restatement of Torts (§ 1 to § 503, inclusive) in 1965; Volume 3 (§ 504 to § 707 A) in 1977; and Volume 4 (§ 708 to the end) in 1979. The Institute released the Second Restatement of Contracts in 1981.

# Glossary

An *assault* is a willful attempt or threat to inflict injury upon another person. An assault may be both a **crime** and a **tort**. Under the law of torts, an assault is an act that causes the victim to be fearful of harmful or offensive contact. Accordingly, an assault may take place without actual contact or bodily harm to the other. Though assault is frequently used to describe the act of applying illegal force to another, such an act would more appropriately be termed a battery.

*Assumption of risk* is a doctrine of law which holds that a person may not recover damages for an injury caused when the individual voluntarily exposes himself to a known danger.

A *battery* is an intentional and unwanted physical contact with another person and which harms the other person or is offensive to him or her. A battery is a completed **assault**. Like assault, a battery may subject a person to criminal charges as well as to liability under the law of torts.

*Chattel* is the term used in law to refer to an article of personal property. By definition, a chattel is property that can be moved from one place to another. The law distinguishes chattel from real property, which is fixed in one location and cannot be moved.

A *civil case* is an action or lawsuit brought to enforce, redress, or protect private rights. The term "civil case" encompasses all actions other than criminal proceedings.

*Common law* is frequently used to refer to the judgments and decisions of the courts. The common law is distinguished from statutory law, which consists of the laws adopted by legislatures. The term "at common law" makes specific reference to the judgments that enforced the usages and customs prevalent in England in times before and contemporaneous with the colonization of America. When used in that sense, "common law" refers to the laws of England and the American colonies before the American Revolution.

A *contract* is an agreement between two or more persons that creates an obligation, on the part of each person, to do a particular thing or refrain from doing something. A contract may be either written or oral.

*Contributory negligence* is a failure on the part of a complaining person to exercise ordinary care under circumstances where the individual has suffered an injury and the injury can be attributed both to the actions of that individual as well as to the negligent actions of another.

*Conversion* is any unauthorized act that deprives a person of his property permanently or for an indefinite time.

A *crime* is any act done in violation of the duties that an individual owes to the community. A crime is a violation of the penal law established by a state or by the federal government.

*Defendant* is the term used to refer to the person or party against whom relief or recovery is sought in a lawsuit or, in a criminal case, the accused.

*Fraud* is a false representation of a matter of fact; an intentional perversion of truth so as to induce another person to rely on the false representation and surrender a legal right or something of value.

An *integrated agreement* is a writing adopted by the parties to an agreement as the final and complete expression of the terms to which the parties agree.

An *intentional tort* is a tort or wrong committed by a person who intends to do an act which the law has declared to be wrong. Intentional torts are in contrast to acts of negligence, which are characterized by a failure to exercise reasonable care. Assault, battery, invasion of privacy, intentional infliction of emotional distress, and false imprisonment are examples of intentional torts.

The *"Mendoza Line,"* named after slick-fielding, no-hit shortstop Mario Mendoza, is the imaginary boundary separating those baseball players who have a batting average above .200 and those who are hitting below .200.

A *naked promise* is a promise that is given without any consideration, equivalent, or reciprocal obligation, and which, for that reason, is generally not enforceable under the law.

*Negligent conduct* is an act or action that in itself is permissible under the law but which is performed without the degree of care appropriate under the circumstances.

An *offeree* is a person to whom a contractual offer is made.

An *offeror* is a person who makes a contractual offer to another.

A *parol contract* is a **contract** that is not set down in writing.

*Plaintiff* is the term used to refer to the person or party who complains or sues in a **civil case**.

A *promisee* is a person to whom a promise has been made.

A *promisor* is a person who makes a promise to another.

*Range of apprehension* is a term used in negligence cases as a gauge of the risks that a **defendant** should have foreseen. In the words of one judge, the "range of apprehension" is the dividing line between reasonable foresight and prophetic vision. The law will normally require a person to anticipate, and act to prevent, those risks to others that are within the range of apprehension. Risks that could only have been anticipated through prophetic vision are, by definition, outside the range of apprehension.

*Recaption* is the act of taking back goods or **chattel** of which a person has been wrongfully deprived.

*Res ipsa loquitur* is a rule of evidence which means literally, "the thing speaks for itself." Under the rule of *res ipsa loquitur*, the law may infer that an alleged wrongdoer has been negligent under circumstances where: (1) an accident or injury to another would likely not have occurred if there had not been some form of negligence, and (2) the thing that caused the accident or injury was under the control or management of the alleged wrongdoer.

The *Second Restatement of Contracts* is the compilation of legal principles and supporting commentaries in the field of contract law. The Second Restatement of Contracts was published under the auspices of the American Law Institute in 1981.

The *Second Restatement of Torts* is the compilation of legal principles and supporting commentaries in the field of tort law. The Second Restatement of Torts was completed in 1979. Like the Second Restatement of Contracts, the Second Restatement of Torts was published under the auspices of the American Law Institute.

The *Statute of Frauds* is a much celebrated English law adopted in the year 1677 and repealed in 1954. The Statute of Frauds has been adopted, with various modifications, in virtually every state in the United States. In general, the Statute of

Frauds prevents the enforcement of certain types of contracts unless there is a signed document providing evidence of the agreement.

A *tort* is a legal wrong committed by an individual or a legal entity upon another or upon the property of another. A tort typically involves the invasion of some legal right of a person or the violation of a duty owed to another.

A *tortfeasor* is an individual or entity that commits a **tort**.

*A tortious act* is conduct that subjects a person to liability under the principles of the law of torts. To establish an act as tortious, a person must prove that (1) an act was committed in violation of the law of torts, and (2) there were definite damages or harm that resulted from the act.

*Trespass* is any unauthorized entry upon or invasion of the private premises or land of another.

The *West Coast Offense* is an offensive scheme popular in the National Football League. The West Coast Offense, which was conceived largely by former San Francisco 49ers head coach Bill Walsh, relies on a preponderance of swing passes and short throws. With the West Coast Offense, passing plays set up running plays rather than vice versa.

# Section 1:

# **Tort Cases**

# Intentional Torts

## *Apprehension of Offensive Contact*

### <u>The Threat of a Kiss</u>

#### <u>Situation</u>

Pam Postema began working as a professional baseball umpire in 1977. In 1981, Postema was promoted to the Double A Texas League, becoming the first woman ever to umpire a professional baseball game above the Class A minor leagues. From 1983 to 1986, Postema umpired in the AAA Pacific Coast League. Other milestones followed swiftly. In 1987, she was hired by the Triple-A Alliance of Professional Baseball Clubs. She was behind the plate for the first Triple-A Minor League All-Star Game, held in 1989. She also umpired major league spring training games in 1988 and 1989. Along the way, however, Postema also endured the indignities that came from being a woman in a profession that could be hostile to women. During a 1988 spring training game, Pittsburgh Pirates manager Chuck Tanner asked Postema if she would like a kiss.

#### <u>Issue</u>

Did Chuck Tanner's question constitute a **tortious act**?

#### <u>Analysis</u>

Throughout her umpiring career, Postema was engaged in a constant struggle to succeed in a man's world. If there was one way to humiliate her, it would have been to kiss her while she was trying to perform her job. Under § 19 of the Restatement of Torts, a bodily contact is offensive if it offends a reasonable sense of personal dignity. There is no question that a kiss from Tanner would have offended Postema's sense of personal dignity. However, Tanner did not perform the act. Without bodily contact, there would be no battery.

The issue then becomes whether Tanner caused apprehension in Postema of potentially offensive or harmful contact and hence committed an assault. If the threat of a kiss on the field of play did not cause Postema to become apprehensive, it certainly would have been offensive to her. Nonetheless, Tanner's words, by themselves, would not have amounted to a tort. Section 31 of the Restatement makes it clear that mere words do not amount to an assault unless there are other acts or circumstances that would have put a person in reasonable apprehension of an imminent harmful or offensive contact.

## Source

*Postema v. National League of Professional Baseball Clubs*, 799 F.Supp. 1475 (1992).

## References

RESTATEMENT (SECOND) OF TORTS §§ 19, 31 (1965).

### § 19. What Constitutes Offensive Contact

A bodily contact is offensive if it offends a reasonable sense of personal dignity.

### § 31. Threat by Words

Words do not make the actor liable for assault unless together with other acts or circumstances they put the other in reasonable apprehension of an imminent harmful or offensive contact with his person.

# Noodles Zupo

## Situation

While warming up a pitcher before the start of a game, Baltimore Orioles catcher Frank "Noodles" Zupo began faking throws in the direction of Ed Hurley and the other umpires working the game. Hurley was not amused. He warned Zupo to stop. Feeling a bit frisky, Zupo ignored the warning and resumed his antics. Hurley promptly ejected him from the field.

## Issue

Did Zupo's actions constitute an assault?

## Analysis

Zupo apparently bore no personal hostility toward the umpires and was probably not motivated by a desire to offend them. His actions seemed intended only for his own amusement and, possibly, the amusement of his teammates. Nonetheless, the potential for a tort existed. According to § 34 of the Restatement of Torts, neither personal hostility nor a desire to offend are required for an assault to be committed.

Zupo may not have intended to actually throw the baseball at Hurley, but if there was a chance that the ball could have slipped out of Zupo's hand, § 28 of the Restatement of Torts would come into play. By faking a throw, Zupo had the intent, at least, of putting Hurley in apprehension of contact. Under § 28, if Hurley was aware that Zupo did not intend to throw the ball but was nonetheless fearful that the ball might slip out of Zupo's hand, Zupo would have been liable for assault.

## Source

Rich Marazzi and Len Fiorito, *Aaron to Zuverink: A Nostalgic Look at the Baseball Players of the Fifties* (New York: Stein and Day, 1982), 266.

## References

RESTATEMENT (SECOND) OF TORTS §§ 21, 28, 34 (1965).

## § 21. Assault

(1) An actor is subject to another for assault if:

    (a) he acts intending to cause a harmful or offensive contact with the person of the other or a third person, or an imminent apprehension of such a contact, and

    (b) the other is thereby put in such imminent apprehension.

(2) An action which is not done with the intention stated in Subsection (1, a) does not make the actor liable to the other for an apprehension caused thereby although the act involves an unreasonable risk of causing it and, therefore, would be negligent or reckless if the risk threatened bodily harm.

## § 28. Apprehension of Unintended Bodily Contact

If the actor intends merely to put the other in apprehension of a bodily contact, he is subject to liability for an assault to the other if the other, although realizing that the actor does not intend to inflict such a contact upon him, is put in apprehension of the contact.

## § 34. Personal Hostility

To make the actor liable for an assault under the rule stated in § 21, it is not necessary that the actor be inspired by personal hostility or desire to offend.

# Meeting on the Mound

## Situation

In 1995, a 27-year-old bond trader named John Murray ran onto the baseball diamond at Wrigley Field immediately after Chicago Cubs relief pitcher Randy Myers had given up a two-run home run to Houston Astros pinch hitter James Mouton. Mouton's homer gave the Astros a 9-7 lead and jeopardized the Cubs' bid for one of the four spots in the National League playoffs. No sooner had Mouton's blast cleared the fence than Murray leaped from the stands and ran toward the 6'1", 230-pound Myers. As Murray approached, it looked to the Cubs pitcher like Murray was reaching for a weapon. "I made sure his hands didn't go into his waistband and pull out a knife or a gun," Myers said later. Myers wrestled Murray to the ground. Wrigley Field security officers then escorted Murray to a local police station for booking.

## Issue

Under the law of torts, was John Murray liable for the tort of assault or the tort of battery?

## Analysis

An assault is an act that creates a reasonable apprehension of harmful or offensive contact. The act must be intentional, and it must create a well-founded fear of peril. Myers frustrated what was apparently an attempt by Murray to strike him. Clearly, however, Myers was apprehensive, especially because he thought Murray might have a gun. Under § 23 of the Restatement of Torts, Murray would be subject to liability for assault. The fact that Myers successfully frustrated Murray does not diminish the level of liability. Murray intentionally entered the playing field. Myers' fear of peril was well-founded. Police charged Murray with assault and disorderly conduct.

## Source

"Cubs Pitcher Is Attacked by Spectator," *The Washington Post*, 29 September 1995, D1, D8.

## References

RESTATEMENT (SECOND) OF TORTS §§ 21, 23 (1965).

### § 21. Assault

(1) An actor is subject to another for assault if:

   (a) he acts intending to cause a harmful or offensive contact with the person of the other or a third person, or an imminent apprehension of such a contact, and

   (b) the other is thereby put in such imminent apprehension.

(2) An action which is not done with the intention stated in Subsection (1, a) does not make the actor liable to the other for an apprehension caused thereby although the act involves an unreasonable risk of causing it and, therefore, would be negligent or reckless if the risk threatened bodily harm.

### § 23. Termination of Attempt After Other's Knowledge

If the actor has so acted as to put another in apprehension of an immediate and harmful or offensive contact, he is subject to liability for an assault although he thereafter terminates his attempt or it is frustrated.

# The Threat of Crawling Things

## Situation

Phil Rizzuto was the starting shortstop for the New York Yankees during some of the most successful years in the team's dynasty. Aside from three years lost to service in the Navy during World War II, Rizzuto played for the Yankees from 1941 to 1956. Though fearless at bat and in the field, Rizzuto was laden with phobias, particularly the fear of bugs, insects, and rodents. It didn't take long for teammates to discover a wide range of pranks that would cause Rizzuto to run in fright. During the era in which Rizzuto played, infielders would leave their gloves on the playing field after an opponent's batters had been retired to end an inning. Early in his career, Rizzuto followed this custom, until he became the victim of several disturbing practical jokes. One time, unbeknownst to Rizzuto, one of his teammates placed a dead mouse inside the shortstop's glove as it lay on the field. Upon returning to his shortstop position, Rizzuto inserted his left hand into the glove, only to find the mouse. He threw his glove as high as he could in the air and refused to touch it until a teammate removed the mouse. Fellow Yankees would also hang a rubber snake on a string above Rizzuto's locker in the Yankee clubhouse. After a game, while Rizzuto was taking off his uniform, one of the players would slowly let out the string so that the snake would gradually appear at eye level in front of Rizzuto. Upon catching glimpse of the snake, Rizzuto would run away in terror.

## Issue

Did the conduct of Rizzuto's teammates, in playing "practical jokes" on the shortstop, constitute a tort?

## Analysis

It is apparent that, when it came to snakes and mice, Rizzuto was not a person of ordinary courage. Under the rule stated in § 21 of the Restatement of Torts, an assault would be committed whenever one of Rizzuto's "playful" teammates hung a snake, stuffed a mouse in Rizzuto's glove, or performed any other act that was intended to put Rizzuto in fear of an immediate harmful or offensive contact. The fact that Rizzuto had an apparently abnormal fear of snakes and rodents would not absolve his teammates from liability. Under § 27 of the Restatement of Torts, Rizzuto's teammates would have been liable for an assault even though the sight of a snake or a mouse may not have caused similar apprehension in others.

The two essential elements of an assault, intent to cause apprehension and an imminent apprehension on the part of Rizzuto, would be present. Under § 25 of the Restatement, Rizzuto's teammates would be liable for assault even if they did not directly inflict the offensive or harmful contact themselves. Section 25 recognizes that the apprehension could result from an inanimate object, such as a mechanical buzzer that sounds like a rattlesnake, a rubber toy that has the appearance of a real snake, or some force of nature.

Additionally, a court may well have found that, in view of Rizzuto's extreme fear of mice and snakes, the practical jokes amounted to purposeful and outrageous conduct. If that proved to be the case, under § 46 of the Restatement, Rizzuto's teammates would be liable for the emotional distress inflicted.

## Source

Peter Golenbock, *Dynasty: The New York Yankees 1949–1964* (Englewood Cliffs, NJ: Prentice-Hall, Inc., 1975), 43-45.

## References

RESTATEMENT (SECOND) OF TORTS §§ 21, 25, 27, 46 (1965).

### § 21. Assault

(1) An actor is subject to another for assault if:

    (a) he acts intending to cause a harmful or offensive contact with the person of the other or a third person, or an imminent apprehension of such a contact, and

    (b) the other is thereby put in such imminent apprehension.

(2) An action which is not done with the intention stated in Subsection (1, a) does not make the actor liable to the other for an apprehension caused thereby although the act involves an unreasonable risk of causing it and, therefore, would be negligent or reckless if the risk threatened bodily harm.

### § 25. Source of Danger

To make the actor liable for an assault the actor need not have put the other in apprehension that the actor will himself inflict a bodily contact upon him.

## § 27. Unreasonable Character of Apprehension

If an act is intended to put another in apprehension of an immediate bodily contact and succeeds in doing so, the actor is subject to liability for an assault although his act would not have put a person of ordinary courage in such apprehension.

## § 46. Outrageous Conduct Causing Severe Emotional Distress

(1) One who by extreme and outrageous conduct intentionally or recklessly causes severe emotional distress to another is subject to liability for such emotional distress, and if bodily harm to the other results from it, for such bodily harm.

(2) Where such conduct is directed at a third person, the actor is subject to liability if he intentionally or recklessly causes severe emotional distress:

    (a) to a member of such person's immediate family who is present at the time, whether or not such distress results in bodily harm, or

    (b) to any other person who is present at the time, if such distress results in bodily harm.

# *Battery*

## "Basketball-brawl" at Auburn Hills

### Situation

With only 45 seconds left in a November 19, 2004 contest between the Indiana Pacers and the Detroit Pistons at the Palace of Auburn Hills in Michigan, 6'7" Pacers forward Ron Artest intentionally fouled Detroit center Ben Wallace in an effort to keep him from scoring. Wallace retaliated by pushing Artest. Players from both teams immediately swarmed the basketball court. While officials tried to restore control, Artest took advantage of the lull to lie down on the scorer's table. He grabbed a pair of headphones from a member of a broadcast crew and placed the headphones around his head. According to onlookers, the sight of Artest lounging on the scorer's table infuriated Piston fans. Sensing trouble, a player's agent in the area urged Artest to go into the locker room. "I kept yelling at Ron to get his [butt] out of there," Steve Kauffman said, but "all he did was smile at me." The trouble quickly escalated. Wallace threw a towel at Artest. A fan then threw a plastic cup containing beer, hitting Artest in the face. In response, Artest leaped into the stands and began pummeling a 26-year-old male spectator. While striking the man, Artest asked him, "Did you do it?" "No, man. No!" the fan responded.

### Issue

Assuming Artest had properly identified the person who hit him with the beverage cup, was he justified in striking the individual with his fists?

### Analysis

The provocation of being hit with a plastic cup does not legally allow Artest to retaliate. Had the threat to Artest continued, he would have been justified in meeting force with force. However, there is no legal privilege that would permit Artest, after being hit with a cup, to pummel the offender, even if he had correctly identified the person who threw the cup. Artest has a legal right to defend himself. Under § 63 of the Restatement of Torts, he would have been justified in using appropriate force to defend himself if he reasonably believed that additional harmful or offensive contact was about to happen. Similarly, under § 67 of the Restatement, if Artest reasonably believed the fan would inflict further harmful contact, he could have yelled threatening words to the fan in order to deter additional contact. However, there was no indication that the offending fan was poised to inflict further harm. Once the threat subsided, it was not permissible for Artest to continue the altercation, utter threats, or retaliate with his fists. The only response legally available to him was to walk away.

## Source

"Pistons' and Pacers' Brawl Spills Into Crowd," *The N.Y. Times*, 20 November 2004, D1.

## References

RESTATEMENT (SECOND) OF TORTS §§ 63, 67 (1965).

### § 63. Self-Defense by Force Not Threatening Death or Serious Bodily Harm

(1) An actor is privileged to use reasonable force, not intended or likely to cause death or serious bodily harm, to defend himself against unprivileged harmful or offensive contact or other bodily harm which he reasonably believes that another is about to inflict intentionally upon him.

(2) Self-defense is privileged under the conditions stated in Subsection (1), although the actor correctly or reasonably believes that he can avoid the necessity of so defending himself,

   (a) by retreating or otherwise giving up a right or privilege, or

   (b) by complying with a command with which the actor is under no duty to comply or which the other is not privileged to enforce by the means threatened.

### § 67. Assault or Imprisonment in Self-Defense

The actor is privileged intentionally to confine another or to put him in apprehension of a harmful or offensive contact for the purpose of preventing him from inflicting a harmful or offensive contact or other bodily harm upon the actor, under the same conditions which create a privilege to inflict a harmful or offensive contact or other bodily harm upon the other for the same purpose.

# Pedro and Old Man Zim

## Situation

In Game 3 of the 2003 American League championship series between the New York Yankees and the Boston Red Sox, Boston pitcher Pedro Martinez threw the Yankees' 72-year-old bench coach, Don Zimmer, to the ground during a melee that erupted in the fourth inning. In the top of the fourth, Martinez threw a pitch behind the head of Yankees outfielder Karim Garcia. The umpire ruled that the pitch hit Garcia in the back and awarded him first base. With the Yankees' Alfonso Soriano at bat, Garcia took off for second base, slid hard, and knocked Boston second baseman Todd Walker off his feet. Walker and Garcia began shoving each other. Players from both dugouts streamed onto the playing field before the umpires restored order. In the bottom half of the inning, Yankees pitcher Roger Clemens threw a fastball up and in to Red Sox slugger Manny Ramirez, prompting Ramirez to yell at Clemens. The shouting escalated and both benches again cleared. The feisty Zimmer headed for Martinez, 41 years younger, and lunged at him. Martinez avoided Zimmer's lunge and, using both hands, grabbed the veteran coach by his head. Martinez then tossed Zimmer to the ground. Zimmer landed face down on the field and rolled over. He suffered only a cut on his nose but, after the game, was taken away on a stretcher for examination at a Boston hospital. Afterwards, Martinez said that Zimmer tried to hit him, so he pushed the coach away. The 31-year-old right-hander also commented that he would never attempt to hit Zimmer.

## Issues

In lunging at Pedro Martinez, was Don Zimmer liable for the tort of assault?

Was the action of Martinez, in pushing Zimmer away, privileged?

## Analysis

Whatever Zimmer's intent, his lunge toward Martinez did not strike fear in Martinez or cause any significant degree of apprehension. Martinez seemed to recognize Zimmer's act for what it was—a somewhat amusing effort by a feisty senior citizen to adhere to baseball's unwritten code of defending one's teammates. If it had been a younger man lunging at Martinez, the act might have caused apprehension, thereby rising to the level of an assault.

Martinez's actions, in turn, were entirely consistent with the law of self-defense. He did what was necessary to deflect Zimmer's lunge, using only force that was reasonable. Martinez could have chosen to back away from Zimmer but, under § 63 of the Restatement of Torts, he was not obligated to do so. Martinez's actions in self-defense were privileged. He was not liable in tort.

## Source

Tyler Kepner, "On Frenzied Day at Fenway, Yanks Survive; Zimmer Is Sent Tumbling, Fight Breaks Out in Bullpen and, Meanwhile, Clemens Tops Martinez," *The N.Y Times*, 12 October 2003, Sec. 8, 1.

## References

RESTATEMENT (SECOND) OF TORTS §§ 21, 63 (1965).

### § 21. Assault

(1) An actor is subject to another for assault if:

   (a) he acts intending to cause a harmful or offensive contact with the person of the other or a third person, or an imminent apprehension of such a contact, and

   (b) the other is thereby put in such imminent apprehension.

(2) An action which is not done with the intention stated in Subsection (1, a) does not make the actor liable to the other for an apprehension caused thereby although the act involves an unreasonable risk of causing it and, therefore, would be negligent or reckless if the risk threatened bodily harm.

### § 63. Self-Defense by Force Not Threatening Death or Serious Bodily Harm

(1) An actor is privileged to use reasonable force, not intended or likely to cause death or serious bodily harm, to defend himself against unprivileged harmful or offensive contact or other bodily harm which he reasonably believes that another is about to inflict intentionally upon him.

(2) Self-defense is privileged under the conditions stated in Subsection (1), although the actor correctly or reasonably believes that he can avoid the necessity of so defending himself,

   (a) by retreating or otherwise giving up a right or privilege, or

   (b) by complying with a command with which the actor is under no duty to comply or which the other is not privileged to enforce by the means threatened.

# Uncle Robbie's Grapefruit

## Situation

Wilbert "Uncle Robbie" Robinson, who spent seventeen years in the major leagues as a catcher, was once coaxed into trying to catch a baseball thrown from an airplane. Uncle Robbie's stunt took place in Florida while the Brooklyn Dodgers, whom Robinson then managed, were in spring training. A Dodgers' clubhouse man went up in the airplane, carrying with him two baseballs. The first time the plane flew over the ball park, the clubhouse man miscalculated the speed of the plane. He dropped the baseball a half-mile outside the park. The clubhouse man's timing was no better on the plane's second pass. Again, the ball fell outside the park. With his supply of baseballs exhausted, the clubhouse man was in a quandary. He was reluctant to ask the pilot to land the plane to get more baseballs. In search of an alternative, the clubhouse man spied a sack of Florida grapefruit on the plane. He instructed the pilot to make another pass over the field. This time, throwing a grapefruit instead of a baseball, the clubhouse man's timing was impeccable. From ground level, Uncle Robbie drew a bead on the falling grapefruit, fully expecting a baseball. "I got it, I got it!" Uncle Robbie yelled. The grapefruit landed in Uncle Robbie's glove and, on impact, exploded. The force of the grapefruit knocked Robinson to the ground. Juice and pulp splashed all over his face. In a panic, he yelled, "I'm bleeding to death. Help me!" Sensing Robinson's consternation, onlookers erupted in laughter. When the laughter subsided, those in attendance teased Robinson by calling him "Grapefruit." To Uncle Robbie's dismay, the new moniker endured for the remainder of his career in baseball.

## Issue

In causing Robinson to come in contact with a foreign substance, was the Dodgers' clubhouse man liable for the tort of battery?

## Analysis

Under § 18 of the Restatement of Torts, if one person causes another to come in contact with a foreign substance in a manner which the other will regard as offensive, the actor is liable in tort. Section 18 governs situations in which there is an offense to the dignity of a person resulting from an intentional and unpermitted invasion of his person. Under § 19 of the Restatement, a bodily contact is offensive if it offends a reasonable sense of personal dignity. It would be difficult to imagine a greater indignity for a major league manager than being splashed with grapefruit juice and pulp in front of his players. The critical question would have been whether the invasion of Robinson's person was unpermitted and intentional. The catcher-turned-manager put himself in position to catch a baseball, not a grapefruit. Robinson would surely have declined to participate if he had known the clubhouse man would be dropping a grapefruit. The offense to his dignity was both unpermitted and intentional. The result was a tort.

## Source

Lawrence S. Ritter, *The Glory of Their Times: The Story of the Early Days of Baseball Told by the Men Who Played It* (New York: William Morrow and Company, Inc., 1992), 214–15.

## References

RESTATEMENT (SECOND) OF TORTS §§ 18, 19, 307, 313 (1965).

### § 18. Battery: Offensive Contact

(1) An actor is subject to liability to another for battery if:

(a) he acts intending to cause a harmful or offensive contact with the person of the other or a third person, or an imminent apprehension of such a contact, and

(b) an offensive contact with the person of the other directly or indirectly results.

(2) An act which is not done with the intention stated in Subsection (1, a) does not make the actor liable to the other for a mere offensive contact with the other's person although the act involves an unreasonable risk of inflicting it and, therefore, would be negligent or reckless if the risk threatened bodily harm.

### § 19. What Constitutes Offensive Contact

A bodily contact is offensive if it offends a reasonable sense of personal dignity.

### § 307. Use of Incompetent or Defective Instrumentalities

It is negligence to use an instrumentality, whether a human being or a thing, which the actor knows or should know to be so incompetent, inappropriate, or defective, that its use involves an unreasonable risk of harm to others.

### § 313. Emotional Distress Unintended

(1) If the actor unintentionally causes emotional distress to another, he is subject to liability to the other for resulting illness or bodily harm if the actor:

(a)    should have realized that his conduct involved an unreasonable risk of causing the distress, otherwise than by knowledge of the harm or peril of a third person, and

(b)    from facts known to him should have realized that the distress, if it were caused, might result in illness or bodily harm.

(2)    The rule stated in Subsection (1) has no application to illness or bodily harm of another which is caused by emotional distress arising solely from harm or peril to a third person, unless the negligence of the actor has otherwise created an unreasonable risk of bodily harm to the other.

# An Overdose of Guacamole

## Situation

Detroit Pistons head coach Larry Brown got his start in coaching with the Carolina Cougars of the American Basketball Association. Wherever he coached, Brown was a fan favorite. He was also the kind of coach whom opposing fans seemed to despise. Brown found the fans in San Antonio to be particularly abusive. To retaliate, Brown would take his case to the press. Once, in a moment of pique, he told newspaper reporters, "The only good thing about San Antonio is the guacamole salad." As Brown no doubt intended, the fans in San Antonio took the insult personally. After one game, as Brown and his team headed to the locker room tunnel, some fans sitting in the stands above the tunnel entrance dumped a pile of guacamole on him.

## Issue

Were the fans who dumped guacamole on Larry Brown liable for the tort of battery?

## Analysis

A battery is an intentional contact that is harmful or offensive. The San Antonio fans may not have construed the dumping of guacamole as a battery, but Larry Brown certainly could have. Brown was not injured in the incident. However, the lack of injury does not preclude a finding of battery. If Brown found the contact offensive, the incident would constitute a battery. Under § 19 of the Restatement of Torts, for a contact to be offensive to a person's dignity, it must be one which would offend an ordinary person. The contact must be unwarranted by the social usages prevalent at the time and place at which it is inflicted. Dumping a mound of guacamole on an individual would have been unwarranted by the prevailing social usages. The fans who dumped the guacamole on Brown were liable for the tort of battery.

## Source

Terry Pluto, *Loose Balls: The Short, Wild Life of the American Basketball Association As Told by the Players, Coaches, and Movers and Shakers Who Made It Happen* (New York: Simon and Schuster, 1990), 305–06.

## References

RESTATEMENT (SECOND) OF TORTS §§ 18, 19 (1965).

### § 18. Battery: Offensive Contact

(1)  An actor is subject to liability to another for battery if:

(a)  he acts intending to cause a harmful or offensive contact with the person of the other or a third person, or an imminent apprehension of such a contact, and

(b)  an offensive contact with the person of the other directly or indirectly results.

(2)  An act which is not done with the intention stated in Subsection (1, a) does not make the actor liable to the other for a mere offensive contact with the other's person although the act involves an unreasonable risk of inflicting it and, therefore, would be negligent or reckless if the risk threatened bodily harm.

### § 19. What Constitutes Offensive Contact

A bodily contact is offensive if it offends a reasonable sense of personal dignity.

# A Kiss for Kamieniecki

## Situation

Sunday, July 28, 1991, loomed as a big day in the life of New York Yankees rookie pitcher Scott Kamieniecki. He was scheduled to take the mound against the California Angels. Up to that point, the season had been quite a success for Kamieniecki. Relying on a fastball that traveled more than 90 miles an hour and a decent repertoire of breaking balls, Kamieniecki had posted a record of four wins against two losses. He had compiled a sparkling earned run average of 2.68. Kamieniecki had more incentive than usual to pitch well against the Angels. The Yankee Stadium crowd of 30,000 included his young wife and her parents, who had flown from Michigan for the game. They were sitting in the box seats set aside for Yankee guests. Kamieniecki would soon have more to think about than simply impressing his wife and her parents, however. As he was getting set to pitch to California Angels second baseman Luis Sojo in the top of the second, a twenty-four-year-old exotic dancer named Laurie Stathopoulos, known professionally as Toppsy Curvey, strode onto the baseball field. Upon reaching the pitcher's mound, she planted a big kiss on Kamieniecki's cheek. Kamieniecki, distracted and wearing a sheepish grin, let the baseball fall from his hands. Security guards then came to Kamieniecki's rescue and took Stathopoulos away. When play resumed, Kamieniecki promptly gave up a two-run double to Sojo. The Angels went on to an 8-4 victory. After the game, Kamieniecki said his pitch to Sojo sailed too far out over home plate. He insisted, however, that Stathopoulos's kiss was not the reason. He said he simply did not have his good stuff.

## Issue

Was Stathopoulos liable for the tort of either assault or battery as a result of her actions?

## Analysis

An assault is an act that creates a reasonable apprehension of harmful or offensive contact. The act must be intentional and create a well-founded fear of peril. A battery is intentional contact that is harmful or offensive; it is a completed assault. Only Kamieniecki knows for sure whether Stathopoulos created a reasonable apprehension of harmful or offensive contact. Newspaper accounts reported that the Yankee was left with a smudge of lipstick and a sheepish grin, suggesting amusement more than fright.

When asked about the incident years later, Kamieniecki said that he was neither apprehensive nor afraid. He was surprised, however, because the stripper had first headed toward the Yankees' third baseman and then veered, unexpectedly, toward the pitching mound. He also said that he was embarrassed that the uninvited kiss took place in full view of his wife and in-laws.

Under § 21 of the Restatement of Torts, Stathopoulos would not be liable for assault. Although she did make an unwelcome contact with Kamieniecki, she did not intend the contact to be either offensive or harmful. Her actions apparently did not cause the Yankee pitcher to become apprehensive of harmful contact. Under § 18 of the Restatement, Stathopoulos would not be liable for battery either, and for the same reasons.

---

## Source

Filip Bondy, "Yankees Stripped of Victory," *The N.Y. Times*, 29 July 1991, C1, C3.

## References

RESTATEMENT (SECOND) OF TORTS §§ 18, 19, 21 (1965).

### § 18. Battery: Offensive Contact

(1) An actor is subject to liability to another for battery if:

    (a) he acts intending to cause a harmful or offensive contact with the person of the other or a third person, or an imminent apprehension of such a contact, and

    (b) an offensive contact with the person of the other directly or indirectly results.

(2) An act which is not done with the intention stated in Subsection (1, a) does not make the actor liable to the other for a mere offensive contact with the other's person although the act involves an unreasonable risk of inflicting it and, therefore, would be negligent or reckless if the risk threatened bodily harm.

### § 19. What Constitutes Offensive Contact

A bodily contact is offensive if it offends a reasonable sense of personal dignity.

### § 21. Assault

(1) An actor is subject to another for assault if:

    (a) he acts intending to cause a harmful or offensive contact with the person of the other or a third person, or an imminent apprehension of such a contact, and

(b)   the other is thereby put in such imminent apprehension.

(2)   An action which is not done with the intention stated in Subsection (1, a) does not make the actor liable to the other for an apprehension caused thereby although the act involves an unreasonable risk of causing it and, therefore, would be negligent or reckless if the risk threatened bodily harm.

# Wurst Comes to Worst

## Situation

On July 9, 2003, Pittsburgh Pirates first baseman Randall Simon struck "Guido," the Italian sausage mascot, during the human sausage race that has become a tradition at home games of the Milwaukee Brewers. The race featured four "contestants," each dressed in a costume. In addition to the Italian sausage, there was a hot dog, a bratwurst, and a Polish sausage. The costumes worn by each mascot were top-heavy, weighing fifty pounds and measuring more than eight feet in height.

As Guido passed by the Pirates' dugout, Simon tapped the mascot on its head with a bat, causing the sausage to topple over and bump the hot dog, which also fell to the ground. The woman inside the Italian sausage costume suffered bruised knees, as did the woman dressed as a hot dog. "Wurst Came to Worst," read one newspaper account. According to the same article, on the day after the incident, the Milwaukee County District Attorney's Office "grilled" the hot dog, the Italian sausage, and one independent witness.

When explaining his actions, Simon said that he did not intend to knock the Italian sausage over. His intent, he said, was merely to tap the top of the costume.

## Issues

Was Simon liable for battery against the woman posing as the Italian sausage?

Was he liable for battery against the woman posing as the hot dog?

## Analysis

After the incident, a contrite Simon said that he did not intend to cause any harm. Though he did not intend to knock the Italian sausage over and did not intend to cause bodily harm, he intentionally made contact with the mascot's costume. Simon was liable for a battery against the Italian sausage mascot, based on § 16(1) of the Restatement of Torts. His actions directly caused the sausage mascot to suffer bruised knees. Under § 16(1), where contact that is offensive produces bodily harm, the person initiating the contact is liable for battery even if there was no intention of causing harm.

Simon did not make contact with the hot dog mascot. Nor did he intend to make contact with the hot dog. Nonetheless, he was also liable for battery against the hot dog mascot. Under § 16(2) of the Restatement of Torts, Simon was liable to the hot dog mascot as fully as if he had intentionally made contact. His actions indirectly caused the hot dog mascot to suffer bruised knees.

Immediately after the game, police read Simon his Miranda rights, handcuffed him, and transported him to the Milwaukee County Jail, where he was photographed and fingerprinted. He explained to the police that he had "nudged the Italian sausage in fun." Simon pleaded guilty to disorderly conduct and was fined $432. Displaying both restraint and good humor, neither the Italian sausage mascot nor the hot dog mascot filed suit against Simon for damages.

---

## Source

Amy Shipley, "A Teeny Weenie Fine," *The Washington Post*, 11 July 2003, D1, D5.

## References

RESTATEMENT (SECOND) OF TORTS §§ 8 A, 13, 16, 18, 19, 34 (1965).

### § 8 A. Intent

The word "intent" is used throughout the Restatement of this Subject to denote the fact that the actor desires to cause consequences of his act, or that he believes that the consequences are substantially certain to result from it.

### § 13. Battery: Harmful Contact

An actor is subject to liability to another for battery if:

- (a) he acts intending to cause a harmful or offensive contact with the person of the other or a third person, or an imminent apprehension of such a contact, and

- (b) a harmful contact with the person of the other directly or indirectly results.

### § 16. Character of Intent Necessary

(1) If an act is done with the intention of inflicting upon another an offensive but not a harmful bodily contact, or of putting another in apprehension of either a harmful or offensive bodily contact, and such act causes a bodily contact to the other, the actor is liable to the other for a battery although the act was not done with the intention of bringing about the resulting bodily harm.

(2)  If an act is done with the intention of affecting a third person in the manner stated in Subsection (1), but causes a harmful bodily contact to another, the actor is liable to such other as fully as though he intended so to affect him.

## § 18. Battery: Offensive Contact

(1)  An actor is subject to liability to another for battery if:

    (a)  he acts intending to cause a harmful or offensive contact with the person of the other or a third person, or an imminent apprehension of such a contact, and

    (b)  an offensive contact with the person of the other directly or indirectly results.

(2)  An act which is not done with the intention stated in Subsection (1, a) does not make the actor liable to the other for a mere offensive contact with the other's person although the act involves an unreasonable risk of inflicting it and, therefore, would be negligent or reckless if the risk threatened bodily harm.

## § 19. What Constitutes Offensive Contact

A bodily contact is offensive if it offends a reasonable sense of personal dignity.

## § 34. Personal Hostility

To make the actor liable for an assault under the rule stated in § 21, it is not necessary that the actor be inspired by personal hostility or desire to offend.

# *Invasion of Privacy*

## <u>Good Stuff, Bad Luck</u>

### <u>Situation</u>

Art Ditmar pitched for the New York Yankees in the 1960 World Series against the Pittsburgh Pirates. He started the first and fifth games of the Series, both of which the Pirates won. In the two games, Ditmar yielded six hits and four runs in one and two-thirds innings. However, his statistics were misleading. Coming to Ditmar's defense, Yankees pitching coach Eddie Lopat said, "there is no substitute for experience and stuff and Ditmar had both. But he didn't have any luck."

Game 5 ended Art Ditmar's appearances in the 1960 Series, but it did not end his bad luck. In the seventh game, future Hall-of-Famer Bill Mazeroski unloaded a ninth-inning, game-winning home run off Yankee pitcher Ralph Terry. On radio, play-by-play announcer Chuck Thompson told a different story. As Mazeroski's hit cleared the left field fence, Thompson told the listening audience that the homer had been hit off Art Ditmar, not Ralph Terry. Thompson explained, "I think I had just seen Ditmar warming up in the bullpen."

Thompson's error might have eased gracefully into the shadows of World Series history if Anheuser-Busch had not selected Thompson's play-by-play as the back-drop for a Budweiser Beer television commercial during the 1985 World Series. The commercial showed customers in a neighborhood bar listening to the radio as Thompson described Mazeroski's dramatic home run. The Budweiser com-mercial ran for the first two games of the 1985 Series. After publication of a newspaper article pointing out Thompson's erroneous reference to Ditmar, Anheuser-Busch took the commercial off the air for the third, fourth and fifth games. Inexplicably, however, the brewery aired the commercial again during Games six and seven. Ditmar sued Anheuser-Busch for invasion of privacy.

### <u>Issue</u>

By replaying the radio broadcast that erroneously attributed the home-run pitch to Art Ditmar, did Anheuser-Busch invade the former pitcher's privacy?

## Analysis

Anheuser-Busch may well have engaged in tortious invasion of privacy when it replayed the commercial. In 1985, Ditmar was 56 years old. The Budweiser commercial came twenty-five years after the original broadcast and more than twenty years after Ditmar had thrown his last pitch in the big leagues. He was living in solitude, well out of the public gaze. Under § 652 B of the Restatement of Torts, one who intentionally intrudes upon the solitude or seclusion of another is subject to liability for invasion of privacy if the intrusion would be offensive to a reasonable person. Similarly, under § 652 E of the Restatement, one who gives publicity to a matter that places another person in a false light is subject to liability for invasion of privacy if the false light would be highly offensive to a reasonable person. For sure, being falsely portrayed as the "goat" of the 1960 World Series was offensive to Ditmar. Nonetheless, he lost his lawsuit. The judge assigned to the case demonstrated little understanding of the significance that Mazeroski's home run holds in baseball lore. However, if the case had been brought in New York, where Mazeroski's home run remains a source of irritation to many, the outcome might have been different.

## Source

*Ditmar v. Needham, Harper, Worldwide, Inc., et al.*, No. C 86-662 (U.S. Dist. Ct., N.D. Ohio) (1986).

## References

RESTATEMENT (SECOND) OF TORTS §§ 580 B, 652 B, 652 E (1977).

### § 580 B. Defamation of Private Persons

One who publishes a false and defamatory communication concerning a private person, or concerning a public official or public figure in relation to a purely private matter not affecting his conduct, fitness or role in his public capacity, is subject to liability, if, but only if, he:

(a)  knows that the statement is false and that it defames the other,

(b)  acts in reckless disregard of these matters, or

(c)  acts negligently in failing to ascertain them.

## § 652 B. Intrusion upon Seclusion

One who intentionally intrudes, physically or otherwise, upon the solitude or seclusion of another or his private affairs or concerns, is subject to liability to the other for invasion of his privacy, if the intrusion would be highly offensive to a reasonable person.

## § 652 E. Publicity Placing Person in False Light

One who gives publicity to a matter concerning another that places the other before the public in a false light is subject to liability to the other for invasion of his privacy, if:

(a) the false light in which the other was placed would be highly offensive to a reasonable person, and

(b) the actor had knowledge of or acted in reckless disregard as to the falsity of the publicized matter and the false light in which the other would be placed.

# Into the Teeth of the Enemy Barrage

## Situation

A writer once fabricated substantial segments of a book that he passed off as a biography of Milwaukee Braves pitcher Warren Spahn. The writer portrayed Spahn as a military hero during World War II, reporting that, during the Battle of the Bulge, Spahn "raced out into the teeth of the enemy barrage." Though Spahn was awarded a Bronze Star for his efforts during the Battle of the Bulge, he did not race "into the teeth of the enemy barrage." The book also reported that Spahn's father taught him to pitch and that his father provided advice to Spahn before he signed his first professional **contract**. Neither statement was true. The writer also inaccurately depicted Spahn's relationship with baseball figures Casey Stengel, Jackie Robinson and Lew Burdette. Spahn sued both the publisher and author for humiliation and mental anguish. He did not want friends and acquaintances to think that he had embellished his war record. Spahn also wanted to correct the notion that a close father-son relationship was essential for a successful career in baseball.

## Issue

Did publication of the inaccurate biography violate Warren Spahn's right of privacy?

## Analysis

Under § 652 E of the Restatement of Torts, one who gives publicity to a matter that places another person in a false light is subject to liability for invasion of privacy if the false light would be highly offensive to a reasonable person. Spahn's complaint with the book, in part, was that some of the passages were overly laudatory. It is not clear that a reasonable person would necessarily have found the passages offensive. As he did so often on the mound, however, Spahn prevailed in court. The court found numerous "factual errors, distortions and fanciful passages" in the purported biography. The court concluded that both the writer and the publisher had shown a careless disregard for the responsibility of the press and ordered them to pay Spahn $10,000 in damages. The decision made it clear that if the biography had been accurate, there would have been no infringement of law. The court stated that if the affairs of an individual fall within the category of current news or information in which the community has a legitimate interest, the right of privacy must yield.

## Source

*Spahn v. Julian Messner, Inc.*, 250 N.Y.S.2d 529 (1964).

## References

RESTATEMENT (SECOND) OF TORTS §§ 552 A, 652 B, 652 D, 652 E (1977).

### § 552 A. General Principle

(1) One who invades the right of privacy of another is subject to liability for the resulting harm to the interests of the other.

(2) The right of privacy is invaded by:

    (a) unreasonable intrusion upon the seclusion of another, as stated in § 652 B; or

    (b) appropriation of the other's name or likeness, as stated in § 652 C; or

    (c) unreasonable publicity given to the other's private life, as stated in § 652 D; or

    (d) publicity that unreasonably places the other in a false light before the public, as stated in § 652 E.

### § 652 B. Intrusion upon Seclusion

One who intentionally intrudes, physically or otherwise, upon the solitude or seclusion of another or his private affairs or concerns, is subject to liability to the other for invasion of his privacy, if the intrusion would be highly offensive to a reasonable person.

### § 652 D. Publicity Given to Private Life

One who gives publicity to a matter concerning the private life of another is subject to liability to the other for invasion of privacy, if the matter publicized is of a kind that:

    (a) would be highly offensive to a reasonable person, and

    (b) is not of legitimate concern to the public.

### § 652 E. Publicity Placing Person in False Light

One who gives publicity to a matter concerning another that places the other before the public in a false light is subject to liability to the other for invasion of his privacy, if:

    (a) the false light in which the other was placed would be highly offensive to a reasonable person, and

(b)   the actor had knowledge of or acted in reckless disregard as to the falsity of the publicized matter and the false light in which the other would be placed.

# To Fax Or Not To Fax

## Situation

In June 1991, the University of Tennessee dismissed assistant football coach Jack Sells. Months after his dismissal, Sells found a way to help a friend, Ron Zook, who was the defensive coordinator for the University of Florida. In the days before Tennessee was to play Florida, Sells took some diagrams of Tennessee's football plays to a Kinko's copy center and paid to have the papers faxed to Zook. Before faxing the documents, a Kinko's attendant examined the diagrams and recognized them as football plays used by Tennessee. Kinko's then alerted the Tennessee athletic department. The incident soon became public knowledge. Unhappy Tennessee football fans began to harass Sells. Sells placed the blame squarely on Kinko's. He sued the company for $3 million dollars, alleging that Kinko's had violated his privacy and damaged his reputation.

## Issue

Under the law of torts, was Kinko's liable for violating Sells' privacy and damaging his reputation?

## Analysis

Section 652 D of the Restatement of Torts provides for tort liability in a situation where one party gives publicity to statements of fact that are not of legitimate concern to the public. The notes published with the Restatement caution readers that the courts have not established with certainty that the liability indicated in § 652 D is consistent with the First Amendment guarantees of freedom of speech and freedom of the press. The Supreme Court case of *Cox Broadcasting Co. v. Cohn* interpreted the First Amendment to say that there can be no recovery for disclosure of facts that are a matter of public record. However, the transaction between Kinko's and Jack Sells was private in nature. Kinko's agreed to fax the papers for Sells, and Sells agreed to pay for the service. Sells did not ask the Kinko's attendant to read the papers—and he clearly did not anticipate that anyone at Kinko's would read them. The lawsuit was resolved when Sells and Kinko's settled out of court.

## Source

"Coach Settles Suit With Kinko's," *The Washington Post*, 29 July 1995, D2.

## References

*Cox Broadcasting Co. v. Cohn*, 420 U.S. 469 (1975).

• RESTATEMENT (SECOND) OF CONTRACTS § 1 (1981).

### § 1. Contract Defined

A contract is a promise or a set of promises for the breach of which the law gives a remedy, or the performance of which the law in some way recognizes as a duty.

• RESTATEMENT (SECOND) OF TORTS §§ 652 D, 652 E (1977).

### § 652 D. Publicity Given to Private Life

One who gives publicity to a matter concerning the private life of another is subject to liability to the other for invasion of privacy, if the matter publicized is of a kind that

(a) would be highly offensive to a reasonable person, and

(b) is not of legitimate concern to the public.

### § 652 E. Publicity Placing Person in False Light

One who gives publicity to a matter concerning another that places the other before the public in a false light is subject to liability to the other for invasion of his privacy, if:

(a) the false light in which the other was placed would be highly offensive to a reasonable person, and

(b) the actor had knowledge of or acted in reckless disregard as to the falsity of the publicized matter and the false light in which the other would be placed.

# Undergrad Grades

## Situation

During basketball player Marcus Camby's undergraduate days at the University of Massachusetts, university officials distributed a copy of Camby's academic record to *The Boston Globe*. To Camby's dismay, the *Globe* published his grades in the newspaper. Camby never authorized the university to release his academic record. Shortly afterward, Camby notified the school that he intended to sue.

## Issue

Was the University of Massachusetts liable in tort to Marcus Camby for unauthorized disclosure of his academic record?

## Analysis

Legal scholar William Prosser has identified four protections that are inherent in the right of privacy. According to Prosser, the right of privacy entitles an individual to protection from: (1) intrusion upon his solitude or into his private affairs; (2) public disclosure of embarrassing private facts; (3) publicity which places a person in a false light in the public eye; and (4) appropriation of the individual's name or picture for the advantage of another person. *The Boston Globe* determined that its subscribers would have an interest in reading about Marcus Camby's grades because he was a prominent athlete. The *Globe* apparently concluded that the intrusion was warranted. Nonetheless, it seems likely that Prosser would have sided with Camby.

It is questionable, however, as to whether the Restatement of Torts would support Camby's position. Section 652 D premises an action for invasion of privacy on a showing that the disclosure is not of legitimate concern to the public and would be highly offensive to a reasonable person. A 1979 Maryland case examined a similar issue raised in a lawsuit filed by six members of the University of Maryland basketball team. At trial, the court ruled against the basketball players. On appeal, the court upheld the decision of the lower court. Relying on comments to § 652 D, the appellate court found that when individuals voluntarily place themselves in the public eye, such as when basketball players agree to play for a prominent university, academic grades and other matters that would otherwise be private become of legitimate interest to the public.

## Source

"Five U-Mass. Players File Suit," *The Washington Post*, 15 December 1995, B4.

## References

*Bilney v. Evening Star Newspaper Co.*, 406 A.2d 652 (Md. Ct. App. 1979).

RESTATEMENT (SECOND) OF TORTS §§ 552 A, 652 D, 652 H (1977).

### § 552 A. General Principle

(1) One who invades the right of privacy of another is subject to liability for the resulting harm to the interests of the other.

(2) The right of privacy is invaded by:

   (a) unreasonable intrusion upon the seclusion of another, as stated in § 652 B; or

   (b) appropriation of the other's name or likeness, as stated in § 652 C; or

   (c) unreasonable publicity given to the other's private life, as stated in § 652 D; or

   (d) publicity that unreasonably places the other in a false light before the public, as stated in § 652 E.

### § 652 D. Publicity Given to Private Life

One who gives publicity to a matter concerning the private life of another is subject to liability to the other for invasion of privacy, if the matter publicized is of a kind that:

   (a) would be highly offensive to a reasonable person, and

   (b) is not of legitimate concern to the public.

### § 652 H. Damages

One who has established a cause of action for invasion of his privacy is entitled to recover damages for:

   (a) the harm to his interest in privacy resulting from the invasion;

   (b) his mental distress proved to have been suffered if it is of a kind that normally results from such an invasion; and

   (c) special damage of which the invasion is a legal cause.

# Inside the Broncos' Locker Room

## Situation

In 1992, Denver Broncos wide receiver Vance Johnson sued Home Box Office for violation of his right of privacy. HBO had broadcast a show titled "Inside the NFL" that contained video scenes from the Broncos' locker room in the aftermath of a 1992 playoff victory. One of the scenes showed the wide receiver after he had removed all of his football gear and before he had dressed. The cameraman who had taken the pictures warned HBO that there were scenes of a naked player. HBO disregarded the warning and included the scenes in its show.

## Issue

In broadcasting naked shots of Vance Johnson as part of "Inside the NFL," was HBO liable for violating Johnson's right of privacy?

## Analysis

For former Supreme Court Justice Louis Brandeis, one of the primary functions of the Constitution of the United States is to protect a person's right to be left alone. Brandeis and other legal scholars have found the right of privacy to be an extension of the constitutional guarantees of life, liberty, and the pursuit of happiness. For these scholars, the right to life includes the right to a quiet existence, out of the public gaze.

The right of privacy protects athletes from emotional injury stemming from unwanted publicity. Under § 652 B of the Restatement of Torts, one who intentionally intrudes, physically or otherwise, upon the solitude or seclusion of another or his private affairs or concerns is subject to liability for invasion of privacy if the intrusion would be highly offensive to a reasonable person. The invasion of privacy suffered by Vance Johnson would likely have been highly offensive to a reasonable person.

Choosing not to contest the matter in court, HBO reached a settlement with Johnson under which it paid a reported $50,000 in damages.

## Source

Martin J. Greenberg and James T. Gray, *Sports Law Practice*, 2nd ed. (Charlottesville, VA: Lexis Law Publishing, 1998), I, 686.

## References

Restatement (Second) of Torts §§ 552 A, 652 B (1977).

### § 552 A. General Principle

(1) One who invades the right of privacy of another is subject to liability for the resulting harm to the interests of the other.

(2) The right of privacy is invaded by:

    (a) unreasonable intrusion upon the seclusion of another, as stated in § 652 B; or

    (b) appropriation of the other's name or likeness, as stated in § 652 C; or

    (c) unreasonable publicity given to the other's private life, as stated in § 652 D; or

    (d) publicity that unreasonably places the other in a false light before the public, as stated in § 652 E.

### § 652 B. Intrusion upon Seclusion

One who intentionally intrudes, physically or otherwise, upon the solitude or seclusion of another or his private affairs or concerns, is subject to liability to the other for invasion of his privacy, if the intrusion would be highly offensive to a reasonable person.

# A Tragic Disclosure

## Situation

The late Arthur Ashe, a former U.S. Open tennis champion and one-time captain of the U.S. Davis Cup team, contracted AIDS as a result of a blood transfusion. The disease ultimately led to Ashe's death in February 1993. During the early stages of his illness, Ashe wished to keep his condition private. Many of his close colleagues in the professional tennis ranks and in the journalistic community were aware of his illness but, out of respect for his wishes, kept it a secret. In April 1992, *USA Today* learned of Ashe's illness. Ashe was 48 years old at the time and long past his days as a professional tennis player. It had been more than six years since he had resigned as captain of the U.S. Davis Cup team. The newspaper carefully considered whether it should publish the news of Ashe's condition. One of Ashe's friends informed the former tennis player that the newspaper was considering running an article on his illness. With that development, Ashe felt he had no option but to break his silence. At a hastily scheduled news conference, Ashe and his wife disclosed that he was suffering from AIDS. Ashe remarked that *USA Today* "had put me in the unenviable position of having to lie if I wanted to protect our privacy." "No one," he said, "should have to make that choice."

## Issue

If *USA Today* had been the first newspaper to publish the news of Ashe's illness, would the newspaper have been liable for unlawful invasion of privacy?

## Analysis

The balancing of an individual's privacy rights against the publication of matters of public interest remains one of the most challenging areas of the law. The task becomes particularly daunting when the issue concerns disclosure of the medical condition of someone such as Arthur Ashe. Under § 552 A of the Restatement of Torts, invasion of one's right of privacy occurs when there is an unreasonable intrusion upon the seclusion of another or unreasonable publicity given to an individual's private life. The intrusion must be substantial and must involve an area in which there is an expectation of privacy. Clearly, Arthur Ashe and his family believed that his medical condition should be regarded as a private matter. Necessarily, however, public figures must accept greater intrusions into their private lives than others. In Ashe's case, an essential area of inquiry would be whether, as of April 1992, he continued to be a public figure. In right of privacy actions, a public figure is broadly defined as anyone who occupies a position or status where public attention is focused upon him as a person. Under that definition, it seems likely that Ashe would have been considered a public figure. For this reason, disclosure of his medical condition would likely not have given rise to a claim for unlawful invasion of privacy.

## Source

Arthur Ashe and Arnold Rampersad, *Days of Glory: A Memoir* (New York: Ballantine Books, 1993), 17.

## References

RESTATEMENT (SECOND) OF TORTS § 313 (1965); §§ 552 A, 652 B (1977).

### § 313. Emotional Distress Unintended

(1) If the actor unintentionally causes emotional distress to another, he is subject to liability to the other for resulting illness or bodily harm if the actor:

    (a) should have realized that his conduct involved an unreasonable risk of causing the distress, otherwise than by knowledge of the harm or peril of a third person, and

    (b) from facts known to him should have realized that the distress, if it were caused, might result in illness or bodily harm.

(2) The rule stated in Subsection (1) has no application to illness or bodily harm of another which is caused by emotional distress arising solely from harm or peril to a third person, unless the negligence of the actor has otherwise created an unreasonable risk of bodily harm to the other.

### § 552 A. General Principle

(1) One who invades the right of privacy of another is subject to liability for the resulting harm to the interests of the other.

(2) The right of privacy is invaded by:

    (a) unreasonable intrusion upon the seclusion of another, as stated in § 652 B; or

    (b) appropriation of the other's name or likeness, as stated in § 652 C; or

    (c) unreasonable publicity given to the other's private life, as stated in § 652 D; or

    (d) publicity that unreasonably places the other in a false light before the public, as stated in § 652 E.

## § 652 B. Intrusion upon Seclusion

One who intentionally intrudes, physically or otherwise, upon the solitude or seclusion of another or his private affairs or concerns, is subject to liability to the other for invasion of his privacy, if the intrusion would be highly offensive to a reasonable person.

# *Infliction of Emotional Distress*

## "Dear Mr. Talbert"

### Situation

In his ground-breaking book, *Ball Four*, pitcher-turned-author Jim Bouton related an incident in which, as part of a baseball promotion, fans in the Seattle Pilots' radio audience were chosen at random to win a cash prize if a Seattle player hit a home run in a selected inning. The prize included a $25,000 bonus if the home run was a grand slam. In one game, Bouton's teammate, pitcher Fred Talbot, hit a grand slam home run in the designated inning, winning $27,500 for a fan in Gladstone, Oregon. With Bouton providing the inspiration, the Seattle bullpen crew conspired to send Talbot a telegram that was purportedly from the fan. The telegram read, "Thank you very much for making our lives so happy, Mr. Talbert. We feel we must share our good fortune with you. A check for $5,000 will be sent to you when the money arrives." Bouton intentionally misspelled Talbot's name to add realism. It was, Bouton revealed, simply another "clever touch." "Mr. Talbert," of course, never received his check for $5,000.

### Issue

Did Fred Talbot have any claim for damages against Jim Bouton for intentionally causing embarrassment and emotional distress?

### Analysis

As Bouton tells the tale, after receiving the bogus telegram, Talbot made plans to buy a motorboat. Talbot may well have felt embarrassed and humiliated by the fake telegram. In some respects, the "Talbert" telegram is similar to a "pot of gold" case from the 1920s. In that case, townspeople convinced a rather gullible maiden that her relatives had buried a pot of gold on the grounds of a certain house. The townsfolk then proceeded to bury a pot containing rocks and dirt on the property. The maiden spent several months digging and, one day, happened upon the pot of rocks. She transported the pot, unopened, to a local bank. With great fanfare, the bank scheduled a ceremony for the opening of the pot. At the ceremony, the maiden opened the pot with great anticipation, only to find the rocks—and no gold. She sued for disappointment and mental suffering and ultimately prevailed in court.

Under § 46 of the Restatement of Torts, if Talbot had pursued a claim against Bouton, he would have been required to demonstrate that: (1) Bouton's conduct was extreme and outrageous; and (2) Talbot had suffered severe emotional distress. It is doubtful that Talbot could have met the burden of proof. By baseball's standards, Bouton's telegram was simply a practical joke of major league proportions.

## Source

Jim Bouton, *Ball Four: My Life and Hard Times Throwing the Knuckleball in the Big Leagues* (Cleveland, Ohio: The World Publishing Company, 1970), 252.

## References

*Nickerson v. Hodges*, 84 So. 37 (1920).

RESTATEMENT (SECOND) OF TORTS §§ 46, 436 A (1965).

### § 46. Outrageous Conduct Causing Severe Emotional Distress

(1) One who by extreme and outrageous conduct intentionally or recklessly causes severe emotional distress to another is subject to liability for such emotional distress, and if bodily harm to the other results from it, for such bodily harm.

(2) Where such conduct is directed at a third person, the actor is subject to liability if he intentionally or recklessly causes severe emotional distress:

    (a) to a member of such person's immediate family who is present at the time, whether or not such distress results in bodily harm, or

    (b) to any other person who is present at the time, if such distress results in bodily harm.

### § 436 A. Negligence Resulting in Emotional Disturbance Alone

If the actor's conduct is negligent as creating an unreasonable risk of causing either bodily harm or emotional disturbance to another, and it results in such emotional disturbance alone, without bodily harm or other compensable damage, the actor is not liable for such emotional disturbance.

# *False Imprisonment*

## Imprisoned at the Polo Grounds

### Situation

As the 1908 baseball season was winding down, the New York Giants played the Chicago Cubs in a game at the Polo Grounds. The Cubs and Giants were tied for the National League lead. The winner of the contest would take a one-game lead in the standings. The game was the most important match-up of the National League season. When the gates outside the Polo Grounds opened before the game, fans surged into the ballpark. Wave after wave of fans passed through the gates. The ushers and security guards were quickly overwhelmed. Fearing that fans already inside the gates would be trampled, the Giants locked the outside gates. The fans who were inside the park found themselves trapped in an enclosed area between the stadium and the outside fence for about an hour. With the outside gates locked, they could not leave. One frustrated fan sued the Giants for false imprisonment.

### Issue

Were Polo Grounds officials liable for the tort of false imprisonment?

### Analysis

Under § 35 of the Restatement of Torts, a person is subject to liability for false imprisonment if he intentionally acts in a way that directly or indirectly results in the confinement of another person and if the other is conscious of the confinement or is harmed by it.

During the trial over the alleged false imprisonment at the Polo Grounds, it was revealed that there was another gate that fans could have used to leave the stadium. However, stadium officials did not tell the fans about the alternate gate. The court found that the Giants' efforts to control the surging crowd, though well-intended, caused the fans to be imprisoned. The simple remedy would have been to tell the crowd about the other exit.

## Historical Note

*The Cubs-Giants game was memorable because of "Merkle's bonehead." In the bottom of the ninth, the Giants had runners on first and third with the score tied and two outs. Fred Merkle was the runner at first. The batter drove the first pitch to center field, bringing home the runner at third. Seeing the winning run score, Merkle stopped halfway between first and second and then, to avoid the surging crowd, headed for the Giants' clubhouse. The Cubs' Johnny Evers called for the ball and, as fans poured onto the field, Evers touched second base to force Merkle. It was the final out of the inning, so the apparent winning run did not count. When the umpires were unable to clear the fans from the field to resume play, they declared the game a tie. The game was slated to be resumed after completion of the regular season schedule. At season's end, the Giants and Cubs were tied for first place. When the two teams met to complete the suspended game, the Cubs beat famed Giants pitcher Christy Mathewson, thereby winning the National League championship.*

---

## Source

*Talcott v. National Exhibition Co.*, 128 N.Y.S. 1059 (1911).

## References

RESTATEMENT (SECOND) OF TORTS §§ 35, 37, 45 (1965).

### § 35. False Imprisonment

(1) An actor is subject to liability to another for false imprisonment if:

    (a) he acts intending to confine the other or a third person within boundaries fixed by the actor, and

    (b) his act directly or indirectly results in such a confinement of the other, and

    (c) the other is conscious of the confinement or is harmed by it.

(2) An act which is not done with the intention stated in Subsection (1, a) does not make the actor liable to the other for a merely transitory or otherwise harmless confinement, although the act involves an unreasonable risk of imposing it and therefore would be negligent or reckless if the risk threatened bodily harm.

### § 37. Confinement: How Caused

If an act is done with the intent to confine another, and such act is the legal cause of confinement to another, it is immaterial whether the act directly or indirectly causes the confinement.

### § 45. Refusal to Release or to Aid in Escape

If the actor is under a duty to release the other from confinement, or to aid in such release by providing a means of escape, his refusal to do so with the intention of confining the other is a sufficient act of confinement to make him subject to liability.

# *Torts Involving Property*

## Trespassing on the Field of Dreams

### Situation

When filming the 1989 Kevin Costner movie, "Field of Dreams," the film's producers carved the magical baseball diamond out of farmland located in Dyersville, Iowa. Most of the baseball diamond was set on property owned by a man named Don Lansing. In order to take advantage of the Iowa sunsets, however, the producers situated the field to the west of Lansing's farmhouse. Lansing's property didn't extend far enough to the west, so the producers had to use a small tract of land from a neighboring farm. The "Field of Dreams" producers signed two contracts, one with Lansing and one with his neighbors, Al and Rita Ameskamp. The infield, right field and part of center field were on Lansing's property. Left field and part of center field were on land owned by the Ameskamps. The commercial success of the movie unexpectedly turned the Iowa baseball diamond into a tourist attraction. Long after the movie was filmed, amateur baseball teams would visit Dyersville to play on the field. Unfortunately, Lansing and the Ameskamps had different ideas on how the field should be used. The Ameskamps turned the management of their property over to an investment banker and proposed to install batting cages and a 1,800-square-foot souvenir stand. Don Lansing objected. To demonstrate his dissatisfaction with the Ameskamps' approach, Lansing began to ban local baseball teams from using his portion of the field.

### Issue

If, in the process of chasing down an errant throw, one of the amateur baseball players ran onto Don Lansing's property without permission, would the player be liable for the tort of **trespass**?

### Analysis

Under § 158 of the Restatement of Torts, a person is liable for trespass if he intentionally enters land belonging to someone else or fails to remove from the land a baseball or any other object that he is under a duty to remove. All of the property owned by Don Lansing would be "off limits" to the Ameskamps and their guests. If a player happened to run onto Lansing's property without permission, it would

be a trespass. Even in the case of insignificant intrusions, such as if an uninvited person hit a ground ball onto the infield, Lansing would suffer a trespass. If a player merely swung his Louisville slugger across the property line and into Lansing's property, the law would say that a trespass has occurred. However, a court is not likely to impose liability unless the trespass has resulted in actual damage to the property.

## Source

"'Field of Dreams': Field of Squabbles," *The Washington Post*, 28 July 1996, D15.

## References

RESTATEMENT (SECOND) OF TORTS §§ 158, 159, 168, 170 (1965).

### § 158. Liability for Intentional Intrusions on Land

One is subject to liability to another for trespass, irrespective of whether he thereby causes harm to any legally protected interest of the other, if he intentionally (a) enters land in the possession of the other, or causes a thing or a third person to do so, or (b) remains on the land, or (c) fails to remove from the land a thing which he is under a duty to remove.

### § 159. Intrusions Upon, Beneath, and Above Surface of Earth

(1) Except as stated in Subsection (2), a trespass may be committed on, beneath, or above the surface of the earth.

(2) Flight by aircraft in the air space above the land of another is a trespass if, but only if, (a) it enters into the immediate reaches of the air space next to the land, and (b) it interferes substantially with the other's use and enjoyment of his land.

### § 168. Conditional or Restricted Consent

A conditional or restricted consent to enter land creates a privilege to do so only in so far as the condition or restriction is complied with.

### § 170. Consent Conditional or Restricted as to Time

A consent given by a possessor of land to the actor's presence on the land during a specified period of time does not create a privilege to enter or remain on the land at any other time.

# A Costly Home Run

## Situation

Safeco Field, home of the Seattle Mariners, opened in July 1999. In the months before the ballpark opened, plumbers and electricians worked feverishly to get the ballpark ready for use. A 39-year-old plumber named Nolan West was assigned to install beer taps at the stadium's refreshment stands. After quitting work one day, West and a friend walked down to the playing field. West carried a baseball bat and a ball. The friend wielded a video camera. While the friend operated the camera, West stood at home plate, tossed the baseball in the air and hit it. With the enthusiasm of a rookie, West circled the bases and then topped off his "round-tripper" with a headfirst slide into home plate. Obviously pleased with his efforts, West delivered the videotape of his "exploits" to a Seattle television station, which played it on the air.

## Issue

Was Nolan West liable for the tort of trespass?

## Analysis

Section 168 of the Restatement of Torts makes it clear that West enjoyed a conditional or restricted consent to enter Safeco Field. His presence was subject to the condition that he restrict his activities to installing the beer taps. Hitting home runs was not within his job description. Under § 170 of the Restatement, West was obligated to leave the ballpark each day once his work was finished. When he decided to stay after work to film his home run, West opened himself up to liability for trespass under § 214 of the Restatement. Section 214 states that a person who exercises a privilege to enter land in an unreasonable manner is subject to liability for any harm that results from his conduct.

Upon learning of West's exploits on the basepaths, his employer, Polar Beer Systems of Santee, California, promptly fired him. The trespass was not without cost to the Mariners. When West hit his "homer," there was a protective tarp covering the infield. In running the bases, West damaged the tarp. The cost of repair was more than $200.

## Source

"Bat, Ball and Videotape Cost Eager Plumber His Stadium Job," *The Washington Post*, 20 March 1999, D2.

## References

RESTATEMENT (SECOND) OF TORTS §§ 168, 170, 214 (1965).

### § 168. Conditional or Restricted Consent

A conditional or restricted consent to enter land creates a privilege to do so only in so far as the condition or restriction is complied with.

### § 170. Consent Conditional or Restricted as to Time

A consent given by a possessor of land to the actor's presence on the land during a specified period of time does not create a privilege to enter or remain on the land at any other time.

### § 214. Liability for Excess; Trespass ab Initio

(1) An actor who has in an unreasonable manner exercised any privilege to enter land is subject to liability for any harm to a legally protected interest of another caused by such unreasonable conduct.

(2) One who properly enters land in the exercise of any privilege to do so, and thereafter commits an act which is tortious, is subject to liability only for such tortious act, and does not become liable for his original lawful entry, or for his lawful acts on the land prior to the tortious conduct.

# Joyriding in Jason's Porsche

## Situation

Shortly after the start of the 2001 baseball season, Chicago Cubs pitcher Jason Bere purchased a brand new silver Porsche 996 priced at $112,000. After buying the car, Bere drove it to Milwaukee, where the Cubs were to play the Brewers in a Saturday night game. Bere left his car with the valet parking service at a downtown Milwaukee hotel. After Bere had departed for the game, a stranger asked an unsuspecting hotel valet for the silver Porsche. The valet delivered Bere's car to the stranger, who got behind the wheel and sped away. An hour later, the stranger drove the car back to the hotel and disappeared on foot.

## Issues

Was the stranger liable for the tort of **conversion** when he drove off in Bere's Porsche?

If Bere had encountered the stranger during the joy ride, could Bere have used force against the stranger in order to reclaim his Porsche?

## Analysis

The joy ride constituted a trespass to **chattel**. As with trespasses to land, however, a court would probably not impose liability unless the trespass resulted in damage to the Porsche.

For reasons unknown, the joyriding stranger did not intend to permanently deprive Bere of his Porsche. If the stranger had kept the Porsche permanently, he would have been liable for the tort of conversion. As § 222 A of the Restatement of Torts suggests, conversion is a severe and aggravated trespass to chattel that permanently deprives the owner of possession. In Bere's case, there was no permanent deprivation. The stranger's actions, therefore, did not rise to the level of conversion.

Under § 105 of the Restatement, if Bere had caught the culprit driving around in the Porsche, the pitcher would have been permitted to use the amount of force necessary to regain possession of the vehicle. However, § 105 would prohibit Bere from using **recaption** as a pretext for exacting punishment. The purpose underlying Bere's use of force could only be to take back his car, nothing more. Additionally, under § 104 of the Restatement, Bere would have been required to first ask the stranger to give the car back before resorting to the use of force, unless the request would have been useless or would have increased the level of danger.

## Source

"Baby, You Can Drive My Car," *The Washington Post*, 7 June 2001, D7.

## References

Restatement (Second) of Torts §§ 101, 104, 105, 222 A, 227 (1965).

### § 101. How Possession Obtained by Other

(1) The use of reasonable force against another for the purpose of recaption is privileged if the other:

    (a) has tortiously taken the chattel from the actor's possession without claim of right, or under claim of right but by force or other duress or fraud, or

    (b) has otherwise tortiously taken the chattel from the actor's possession and is about to remove it from the actor's premises, or

    (c) has received custody of the chattel from the actor and refuses to surrender it or is about to remove it from the actor's premises.

(2) The privilege stated in Subsection (1) also exists against:

    (a) another who knowingly causes the actor to believe that such facts exist, or

    (b) a transferee of the tortfeasor who knows or should know that such facts exist.

### § 104. Necessity of Demand

The use of force against another for the purpose of recaption is not privileged unless the actor first requests the other to give up possession of the chattel, except where the actor correctly or reasonably believes a request to be useless, dangerous to himself or a third person, or likely to defeat the effective exercise of the privilege.

### § 105. Purpose of Actor

Force used against another in effecting a recaption is not privileged unless the force is used for the purpose of regaining possession of the chattel.

## § 222 A. What Constitutes Conversion

(1) Conversion is an intentional exercise of dominion or control over a chattel which so seriously interferes with the right of another to control it that the actor may justly be required to pay the other the full value of the chattel.

## § 227. Conversion by Using Chattel

One who uses a chattel in a manner which is a serious violation of the right of another to control its use is subject to liability to the other for conversion.

# Pat Boone's Blank Check

## Situation

In 1966, when the American Basketball Association announced its plans to locate a team in Oakland, California, entertainer and recording artist Pat Boone agreed to serve as president and minority owner of the team. In exchange for lending his name to the Oakland Oaks, Boone received a 10% stake in the team. During the first year of operation, the team began to experience financial troubles. The majority owner pressured Boone to sign a blank Bank of America check to pay off a team debt. Boone said, "There is no amount written on this check." The owner told him the check would be for either $245,000 or $251,000 but that he couldn't remember the exact amount and would have to fill it in later. Boone called his business manager for advice. The business manager told Boone it would be okay to sign because the other owners had agreed to indemnify him for any losses that he might incur. Boone figured that, if worse came to worst, he could afford to pay the $250,000 anyway. He signed the check. Worse soon came to worst: the Oaks went bankrupt. Boone learned that the Bank of America check bearing his signature had been written in the amount of $1.3 million. Even worse, Boone found that he would not be indemnified for the loss. Boone considered suing the Bank of America to recoup his $1.3 million.

## Issue

Was the Bank of America liable in tort when it cashed Boone's check for $1.3 million?

## Analysis

Boone was perhaps thinking that the bank had engaged in some form of conversion when it cashed his check for $1.3 million. However, § 241 A of the Restatement of Torts makes it clear that conversion of a check or other negotiable instrument involves the element of forgery. Boone willingly signed the blank check, so there was no misconduct on the part of Bank of America. Lacking any evidence of misdeeds by the bank, Boone's lawyer advised against filing a lawsuit.

## Source

Terry Pluto, *Loose Balls: The Short, Wild Life of the American Basketball Association As Told by the Players, Coaches, and Movers and Shakers Who Made It Happen* (New York: Simon and Schuster, 1990), 95–96.

## Reference

RESTATEMENT (SECOND) OF TORTS § 241 A (1965).

### § 241 A. Conversion of Negotiable Instrument

There is conversion of a negotiable instrument when it is paid on a forged indorsement.

# *Fraudulent Misrepresentation*

## <u>No Sugar, No Scholarship</u>

### <u>Situation</u>

Using the alias Joel Ron McKelvey, Ron Weaver was set to play for the University of Texas in the Sugar Bowl on Sunday, December 31, 1995. Listed in the Sugar Bowl program as a 23-year-old, Weaver played defensive cornerback for the Longhorns. The day before the Sugar Bowl game, *The Californian* newspaper, based in Salinas, California, reported that Weaver was playing for Texas under a false identity. After the story broke, and just hours before his big game, Weaver left New Orleans, the site of the Sugar Bowl, without telling his team. Within days, the Austin (Texas) *American-Statesman* reported that Weaver was actually 30 years old and had previously used up all four years of his college eligibility. Unbeknownst to the University of Texas, Weaver had once played college football at Cal State-Sacramento. His college eligibility expired in 1989. After his eligibility expired, Weaver enrolled at Los Angeles Pierce Community College. To conceal his prior college experience, Weaver took both the name and the social security number of an acquaintance, Joel McKelvey. He played two years at the community college under the name "McKelvey." His hard-nosed play at Los Angeles Pierce Community College drew raves from college recruiters, and the University of Texas, among other schools, awarded Weaver a full athletic scholarship. Still using the name McKelvey, Weaver enrolled at Texas in August 1995.

### <u>Issue</u>

Was Weaver liable in tort for misrepresenting his collegiate eligibility?

### <u>Analysis</u>

Under § 525 of the Restatement of Torts, Weaver's actions constituted fraudulent misrepresentation. He misrepresented his age and college eligibility to induce the University of Texas to grant him a scholarship. The Longhorns clearly relied on Weaver's misrepresentation. Section 525 makes it clear that Weaver was liable to the University for the pecuniary loss caused by his misrepresentation.

After the story broke, federal prosecutors launched an inquiry. Weaver was under investigation for possible wire fraud, mail fraud and violation of the social security laws. In the end, he pleaded guilty to a federal charge of misusing social security numbers.

The judge ordered Weaver to repay the University of Texas for his scholarship, which amounted to $5,000.

Once his cover was blown, Weaver quickly fled the University of Texas and, in the process, gave up his scholarship. If the need had arisen, the University could have relied upon § 164 of the Restatement of Contracts as justification for voiding its scholarship agreement with Weaver.

---

## Sources

"Texas Considers Suing Imposter," *The Washington Post*, 3 January 1996, F4.

"Imposter Pleads Guilty," *The Washington Post*, 16 March 1996, B7.

## References

- RESTATEMENT (SECOND) OF TORTS § 525 (1977).

### § 525. Liability for Fraudulent Misrepresentation

One who fraudulently makes a misrepresentation of fact, opinion, intention or law for the purpose of inducing another to act or to refrain from action in reliance upon it, is subject to liability to the other in deceit for pecuniary loss caused to him by his justifiable reliance upon the misrepresentation.

- RESTATEMENT (SECOND) OF CONTRACTS §§ 159, 162, 164 (1981).

### § 159. Misrepresentation Defined

A misrepresentation is an assertion that is not in accord with the facts.

### § 162. When a Misrepresentation Is Fraudulent or Material

(1)  A misrepresentation is fraudulent if the maker intends his assertion to induce a party to manifest his assent and the maker:

(a)  knows or believes that the assertion is not in accord with the facts, or

(b)  does not have the confidence that he states or implies in the truth of the assertion, or

(c)  knows that he does not have the basis that he states or implies for the assertion.

(2) A misrepresentation is material if it would be likely to induce a reasonable person to manifest his assent, or if the maker knows that it would be likely to induce the recipient to do so.

### § 164. When a Misrepresentation Makes a Contract Voidable

(1) If a party's manifestation of assent is induced by either a fraudulent or a material misrepresentation by the other party upon which the recipient is justified in relying, the contract is voidable by the recipient.

(2) If a party's manifestation of assent is induced by either a fraudulent or a material misrepresentation by one who is not a party to the transaction upon which the recipient is justified in relying, the contract is voidable by the recipient, unless the other party to the transaction in good faith and without reason to know of the misrepresentation either gives value or relies materially on the transaction.

# Other Tort Issues

## *Self-Defense*

### <u>Marichal's Mayhem</u>

#### <u>Situation</u>

On August 22, 1965, pitcher Juan Marichal of the San Francisco Giants came to bat in a game against the Los Angeles Dodgers. Hard-throwing Dodgers left-hander Sandy Koufax was on the mound. On one of Koufax's offerings to Marichal, Dodgers catcher John Roseboro mishandled the pitch. The ball hit Roseboro's glove and fell near home plate. Roseboro picked it up and, when returning the ball to Koufax, threw close to Marichal's head. Marichal took exception. He turned toward Roseboro and brought his bat down hard on the catcher's head. Blood streamed from Roseboro's face. Both benches cleared. Only the peace-keeping efforts of Giants center fielder Willie Mays and the umpiring crew prevented a full-scale riot from erupting. Marichal issued an apology of sorts in which he said he thought Roseboro was going to hit him. Marichal claimed he was acting in self-defense. He contended that the throw from Roseboro actually hit him. "It nicked my ear," Marichal explained, adding "I thought he would hit me with his mask so I hit him."

#### <u>Issue</u>

Assuming that Marichal thought Roseboro was going to hit him, can Marichal's act of hitting Roseboro with a bat be justified as self-defense?

#### <u>Analysis</u>

*New York Times* sportswriter Arthur Daley commented, "It's a cinch…that Marichal would have landed in jail if he had perpetrated his outrageous attack at the corner of Market and Powell Streets in San Francisco instead of at Candlestick Park."

It is a fundamental principle of law that a person, whether on a baseball field or at the corner of Market and Powell Streets, is not justified in using force against another unless it is proportional or reasonable to the threat. The law terms this principle "the doctrine of proportionality." The doctrine is reflected in § 70 of the Restatement of Torts, which states that "the actor is not privileged to use any means of self-defense which is intended or likely to cause a bodily harm or confinement in excess of that which the actor correctly or reasonably believes to be necessary for his protection." Marichal may have feared being hit by Roseboro, but his response was not proportional to the threat.

---

## Sources

Arthur Daley, "Crime and Punishment," *The N.Y. Times*, 25 August 1965, 42.

Leonard Koppett, "Marichal Says He Used the Bat to Hit Roseboro in Self-Defense," *The N.Y. Times*, 24 August 1965, 20.

## References

RESTATEMENT (SECOND) OF TORTS §§ 63, 70 (1965).

### § 63. Self-Defense by Force Not Threatening Death or Serious Bodily Harm

(1) An actor is privileged to use reasonable force, not intended or likely to cause death or serious bodily harm, to defend himself against unprivileged harmful or offensive contact or other bodily harm which he reasonably believes that another is about to inflict intentionally upon him.

(2) Self-defense is privileged under the conditions stated in Subsection (1), although the actor correctly or reasonably believes that he can avoid the necessity of so defending himself,

    (a) by retreating or otherwise giving up a right or privilege, or

    (b) by complying with a command with which the actor is under no duty to comply or which the other is not privileged to enforce by the means threatened.

## § 70. Character and Extent of Force Permissible

(1) The actor is not privileged to use any means of self-defense which is intended or likely to cause a bodily harm or confinement in excess of that which the actor correctly or reasonably believes to be necessary for his protection.

(2) The actor may be privileged in self-defense to do an act which is intended to put another in immediate apprehension of a harmful or offensive contact or other bodily harm or confinement, which is in excess of that which the actor is privileged to inflict, if his act is intended and reasonably believed by him to be likely to do no more than to create such an apprehension.

# Ruben's Retreat

## Situation

In a 1956 game between the New York Giants and the Milwaukee Braves, Giants pitcher Ruben Gomez threw a pitch that nicked Milwaukee's first baseman Joe Adcock on the wrist. Adcock began walking to first, but then abruptly veered toward Gomez. The 6'4" Adcock towered over Gomez, who stood 6'0". Adcock also enjoyed a 40-pound advantage in weight. In an effort to ward off Adcock, Gomez picked up the baseball and threw it at him. Gomez then fled the field in fright, with Adcock in hot pursuit. Before Adcock could catch up, the pitcher took refuge in the Giants' dugout and remained there until police escorted him back to his hotel room.

## Issue

Was Ruben Gomez liable for the tort of battery for throwing the baseball at Joe Adcock?

## Analysis

In the minds of many, Gomez' action in fleeing from Adcock, instead of fighting him, marked him as gutless. One sportswriter maintained that the stigma diminished Gomez' effectiveness as a pitcher for the rest of his big league career. If there is virtue at all in Gomez' conduct, it lies in the fact that, when throwing the baseball at Adcock, his effort at self-defense was reasonably designed to protect himself from Adcock. Section 63(1) of the Restatement of Torts recognizes self-defense as a proper justification for the use of force against another person. The self-defense argument must be plausible, however. With Joe Adcock closing in on him, Ruben Gomez was clearly acting in self-defense when he threw the baseball at Adcock.

Unlike Juan Marichal's attack on John Roseboro, Gomez' action was proportional to the threat. While it may have been prudent for Gomez to retreat, from a legal perspective, he was not under a duty to do so. Under § 63(2) of the Restatement of Torts, Gomez was "privileged" to occupy the pitching mound and could have continued to do so. However, under the circumstances, the Giants' dugout proved to be a much safer alternative.

## Source

Gerald Eskenazi, "Latest Giants-Dodgers Brawl Brings a Few Others to Mind," *The N.Y. Times*, 23 August 1965, 24.

## Reference

RESTATEMENT (SECOND) OF TORTS § 63 (1965).

### § 63. Self-Defense by Force Not Threatening Death or Serious Bodily Harm

(1) An actor is privileged to use reasonable force, not intended or likely to cause death or serious bodily harm, to defend himself against unprivileged harmful or offensive contact or other bodily harm which he reasonably believes that another is about to inflict intentionally upon him.

(2) Self-defense is privileged under the conditions stated in Subsection (1), although the actor correctly or reasonably believes that he can avoid the necessity of so defending himself,

    (a) by retreating or otherwise giving up a right or privilege, or

    (b) by complying with a command with which the actor is under no duty to comply or which the other is not privileged to enforce by the means threatened.

# *Defense of Property*

## Potent Nine-Iron

### Situation

One early morning in 2001, Daniel Stevens of Baltimore approached John Lazzell, a sixty-year-old golf pro at Rocky Point Golf Club in Essex, Maryland, as Lazzell was getting ready for a tournament at the club. Brandishing a gun, Stevens forced Lazzell to open the safe in the pro shop. Lazzell feigned feeling sick. The ploy distracted Stevens long enough for Lazzell to pick up a nine-iron and swing it at Stevens. The force of the nine-iron knocked Stevens down. The two men then struggled for the gun. During the struggle, the gun discharged and Stevens was wounded in the leg. Stevens then fled the scene. Lazzell called the police, who quickly arrived and found Stevens out on the course.

### Issue

Was Lazzell's use of a nine-iron to protect the contents of the pro shop's safe privileged?

### Analysis

Under § 106 of the Restatement of Torts, the use of force against another for the purpose of recaption is privileged so long as the means used are not in excess of those which the actor correctly or reasonably believes to be necessary to effect the recaption and are not intended or likely to cause death or serious bodily harm. Swinging a nine-iron at the intruder was proportional to the harm threatened. Lazzell's actions were privileged.

---

### Source

Kathy Orton, "Club Pro Quells Armed Man," *The Washington Post*, 21 June 2001, D9.

### References

Restatement (Second) of Torts §§ 104, 105, 106 (1965).

## § 104. Necessity of Demand

The use of force against another for the purpose of recaption is not privileged unless the actor first requests the other to give up possession of the chattel, except where the actor correctly or reasonably believes a request to be useless, dangerous to himself or a third person, or likely to defeat the effective exercise of the privilege.

## § 105. Purpose of Actor

Force used against another in effecting a recaption is not privileged unless the force is used for the purpose of regaining possession of the chattel.

## § 106. Amount of Force Permissible

The use of force against another for the purpose of recaption is not privileged unless the means employed are:

(a) not in excess of those which the actor correctly or reasonably believes to be necessary to effect the recaption, and

(b) not intended or likely to cause death or serious bodily harm.

# *Assumption of Risk*

## A Vicious Hook

### Situation

While playing a golf course in Georgia, Brannon Morris hit a vicious hook off the tee. The ball flew off at a seventeen-degree angle and struck another golfer, F. W. Rose, who was standing 125 yards away on an adjacent fairway. Morris did not give warning when his shot went astray. Rose faulted Morris for failing to yell "Fore." Rose sued, seeking compensation for his injuries.

### Issue

Was Morris liable in tort for hitting Rose with the golf ball?

### Analysis

The court ruled in favor of Morris. In the court's view, being hit with a golf ball, even from an adjacent hole, was a risk that Rose assumed when he stepped on the golf course. The court's decision was consistent with § 496 A of the Restatement of Torts. That section states the doctrine of **assumption of risk**, *i.e.*, a plaintiff who voluntarily assumes a risk of harm arising from the negligent or reckless conduct of the **defendant** cannot recover for such harm. In the court's view, because Rose assumed the risk of injury when he stepped onto the golf course, it was immaterial whether Morris gave fair warning of his errant shot.

---

### Source

*Rose v. Morris*, 104 S.E.2d 485 (1958).

### References

RESTATEMENT (SECOND) OF TORTS §§ 301, 328 A, 496 A, 496 D (1965).

## § 301. Effect of Warning

(1) Except as stated in Subsection (2), a warning given by the actor of his intention to do an act which involves a risk of harm to others does not prevent the actor from being negligent.

(2) The exercise of reasonable care to give reasonably adequate warning prevents the doing of an act from being negligent, if:

   (a) the law regards the actor's interest in doing the act as paramount to the other's interest in entering or remaining on the area endangered thereby, or

   (b) the risk involved in the act, or its unreasonable character, arises out of the absence of warning.

## § 328 A. Burden of Proof

In an action for negligence the plaintiff has the burden of proving

   (a) facts which give rise to a legal duty on the part of the defendant to conform to the standard of conduct established by law for the protection of the plaintiff,

   (b) failure of the defendant to conform to the standard of conduct,

   (c) that such failure is a legal cause of the harm suffered by the plaintiff, and

   (d) that the plaintiff has in fact suffered harm of a kind legally compensable by damages.

## § 496 A. General Principle [of Assumption of Risk]

A plaintiff who voluntarily assumes a risk of harm arising from the negligent or reckless conduct of the defendant cannot recover for such harm.

## § 496 D. Knowledge and Appreciation of Risk

Except where he expressly so agrees, a plaintiff does not assume a risk of harm arising from the defendant's conduct unless he then knows of the existence of the risk and appreciates its unreasonable character.

# Third-Grade Defendant

## Situation

During a Little League baseball game in Wallingford, Connecticut in 1995, a nine-year-old pitcher, then in the third grade, threw a wild pitch that struck a spectator. The spectator, Carol LaRosa, and her husband sued the little leaguer for $15,000. Carol LaRosa claimed to have suffered facial injuries that required sixty stitches and left her with headaches and a scar on her jaw. LaRosa accused the pitcher of being careless. She claimed he failed to warn her that he was throwing the baseball and that he threw the ball at a dangerous speed. LaRosa's husband claimed to have been injured by the resulting disruption in marital relations with his wife.

## Issue

Was the nine-year-old pitcher liable in tort for the injuries suffered by Carol LaRosa?

## Analysis

For reasons unknown, the LaRosas sued only the nine-year-old pitcher and not the Little League organization. The judge ruled that a minor child could not be sued as a sole defendant and dismissed the suit on that basis. When investigating the case, a reporter from *Sports Illustrated* asked the lawyer for Carol LaRosa whether she had assumed the risk of injury. Apparently, LaRosa and her lawyer were of the opinion that she had not assumed the risk. Nonetheless, she had voluntarily engaged in an activity where there was an identifiable potential for injury. LaRosa was capable of assessing the risk. By attending the game, especially one with a nine-year-old pitcher, she would seem to have accepted the risk.

Under § 496 A of the Restatement of Torts, LaRosa likely would not have been awarded compensation for her injuries even if the judge had found the little leaguer to be a proper defendant. With regard to the standard of conduct applicable to the pitcher, § 283 A of the Restatement of Torts would require only that his actions be consistent with those of a child of similar age, intelligence and experience.

## Source

Jack McCallum and Kostya P. Kennedy, "The Windup, the Pitch, the Suit," *Sports Illustrated*, 15 January 1996, 30.

## References

RESTATEMENT (SECOND) OF TORTS §§ 283 A, 496 A, 496 D (1965).

### § 283 A. Children

If the actor is a child, the standard of conduct to which he must conform to avoid being negligent is that of a reasonable person of like age, intelligence, and experience under like circumstances.

### § 496 A. General Principle [of Assumption of Risk]

A plaintiff who voluntarily assumes a risk of harm arising from the negligent or reckless conduct of the defendant cannot recover for such harm.

### § 496 D. Knowledge and Appreciation of Risk

Except where he expressly so agrees, a plaintiff does not assume a risk of harm arising from the defendant's conduct unless he then knows of the existence of the risk and appreciates its unreasonable character.

# Wild Pitch at Wrigley

## Situation

In each of the three years from 1954 to 1956, Chicago Cubs pitcher Bob Rush won 13 games for the Cubs. His earned run average during those three years never exceeded 3.77. In 1957, Rush won only 6 games and lost 16. For every nine innings pitched, he allowed an average of 4.38 runs. It was the kind of year that prompts baseball teams to trade players. In fact, before the next season started, the Cubs did trade Rush to the Milwaukee Braves. Before Rush could get out of Chicago, however, he managed to hit a fan in the head with a wild pitch during a game at Wrigley Field. The fan, David Maytnier, was watching the game from the front row box seats, about ten to fifteen seats to the outfield side of the Cubs' dugout. During the sixth inning, Rush was warming up in the Cubs' bullpen, which was situated in foul territory along the left field line. He unleashed a pitch that went over the head of his bullpen catcher and into the stands. The pitch struck Maytnier in the head. The bullpen catcher that day was Gordon Massa, a Cubs reserve. Massa was 6'3". Even at that height, Massa could not reach Rush's pitch. Maytnier sued Rush and the Cubs for his injuries.

## Issue

Did David Maytnier assume the risk of injury when he went to see the baseball game at Wrigley Field?

## Analysis

As a general rule, the law assumes that spectators at baseball games are aware of the potential for injury from thrown or batted baseballs. If a fan attends a game and is hit by a ball, a court would normally not be inclined to award damages, because the fan assumed a known risk. The case of *Maytnier v. Rush and Chicago National League Ball Club, Inc.* stands as an exception to the general rule. The judge held that Bob Rush and the Cubs were liable. The judge ruled that Maytnier could not have been expected to keep his eye on two baseballs simultaneously, the ball that was in play during the game and the ball that Rush was throwing in the bullpen. In the judge's opinion, it was physically impossible for Maytnier to have seen or anticipated Rush's warm-up pitch while he was watching the action on the field. Maytnier assumed the risk of injury from baseballs that were in play. Consistent with § 496 D of the Restatement of Torts, he did not assume the risk of being hit by an unexpected pitch from the bullpen.

## Source

*Maytnier v. Rush and Chicago National League Ball Club, Inc.*, 225 N.E.2d 83 (1967).

## References

RESTATEMENT (SECOND) OF TORTS §§ 496 A, 496 D (1965).

### § 496 A. General Principle [of Assumption of Risk]

A plaintiff who voluntarily assumes a risk of harm arising from the negligent or reckless conduct of the defendant cannot recover for such harm.

### § 496 D. Knowledge and Appreciation of Risk

Except where he expressly so agrees, a plaintiff does not assume a risk of harm arising from the defendant's conduct unless he then knows of the existence of the risk and appreciates its unreasonable character.

# A Dark and Rainy Road

## Situation

As a young outfielder with the Baltimore Orioles in the late 1980s, Brady Anderson was often overmatched at the plate. In 1988, he hit .198 in 53 games with the Orioles. Anderson did not fare much better in 1989, hitting .207 for the season. He was not alone. Anderson's teammate, Rene Gonzales, a utility infielder, was also struggling to adjust to major league pitching. One night, the two teammates were driving on a darkened Maryland road during a heavy rain. Gonzales was behind the wheel. He was driving at a speed that, given the weather, was dangerously fast. Anderson grew progressively more concerned but refrained from cautioning Gonzales. Finally, Anderson turned to his teammate and said, "You know, Gonzo, if I weren't hitting .198, I'd ask you to slow down."

## Issue

If Rene Gonzales's dangerous driving had resulted in an accident, would Brady Anderson have been found to have assumed the risk of injury?

## Analysis

In sports, as in life, perils abound. Poor batting averages or not, reasonable people usually act to minimize the perils they face. Common sense dictates that people should avoid known dangers. The law expects no less. And the more maturity and experience a person possesses, the greater the expectation that the person will act prudently when there is a possibility of injury. Anderson could have asked "Gonzo" to slow down. He could have offered to drive the car himself. He did neither. By his inaction, Anderson intentionally exposed himself to danger. If there had been an accident, Anderson's conduct would likely have constituted **contributory negligence**, as that term is defined in § 466 of the Restatement of Torts.

Eventually, the two ballplayers arrived safely at their destination. There never arose a need to determine whether Anderson, by continuing to ride with Gonzales, had assumed the risk of injury.

---

## References

RESTATEMENT (SECOND) OF TORTS §§ 466, 478, 496 A (1965).

## § 466. Types of Contributory Negligence

The plaintiff's contributory negligence may be either:

(a)  an intentional and unreasonable exposure of himself to danger created by the defendant's negligence, of which danger the plaintiff knows or has reason to know, or

(b)  conduct which in respects other than those stated in Clause (a), falls short of the standard to which the reasonable man should conform in order to protect himself from harm.

## § 478. Time of Plaintiff's Negligence in Relation to That of Defendant

Except where the defendant has the last clear chance, the plaintiff's contributory negligence bars his recovery, whether it is antecedent or subsequent to that of the defendant, or simultaneous with it.

## § 496 A. General Principle [of Assumption of Risk]

A plaintiff who voluntarily assumes a risk of harm arising from the negligent or reckless conduct of the defendant cannot recover for such harm.

# Slippery Shea

## Situation

Outfielder Elliott Maddox made it to the big leagues with the Detroit Tigers in 1970, largely on the strength of his speed and glove. In his first three years in the American League, Maddox played for three different teams, never living up to the expectations of any of them. Between 1970 and 1973, his highest batting average was .252 and his lowest .217. In 1974, Maddox finally emerged as a productive hitter with the New York Yankees. In 137 games, he hit .303. The following year it was more of the same. After 55 games, Maddox was batting .307. During a night game at rain-soaked Shea Stadium on June 13, 1975, however, he injured his right knee. The injury required three separate surgical procedures to repair. Though Maddox continued to play major league ball until 1980, he never again hit above .300 and retired with a lifetime average of .261. Maddox traced the decline of his career to the knee injury suffered at Shea Stadium. He claimed that, on the night of his injury, the outfield at Shea Stadium was not suitable for play because there were pools of water on the field. Earlier in the game, Maddox had complained to the grounds crew about the dangerous conditions. In the ninth inning, playing center field, he ran to his left in pursuit of a fly ball. As he tried to stop running, Maddox hit a wet spot. His left foot slid. His right foot stuck in a mud puddle, causing his knee to buckle, and ending his season. He sued the city of New York for damages.

## Issue

Would the city of New York, which owned and operated Shea Stadium, be liable in tort for the injury to Elliott Maddox?

## Analysis

The New York State Court of Appeals ruled against Maddox. The court found that Maddox was well aware of the dangerous conditions at Shea Stadium and had voluntarily assumed the risk of playing on the field. Evidence introduced at trial showed that, before suffering his injury, Maddox had voiced concern about the condition of the outfield. With the introduction of that evidence, Maddox's case fell squarely within the assumption of risk doctrine articulated in § 496 A of the Restatement of Torts. As a plaintiff who had voluntarily assumed a known risk, Maddox was precluded from recovering for the harm suffered.

## Source

*Maddox v. City of New York*, 487 N.E.2d 553 (N.Y. 1985).

## References

RESTATEMENT (SECOND) OF TORTS §§ 496 A, 496 D (1965).

### § 496 A. General Principle [of Assumption of Risk]

A plaintiff who voluntarily assumes a risk of harm arising from the negligent or reckless conduct of the defendant cannot recover for such harm.

### § 496 D. Knowledge and Appreciation of Risk

Except where he expressly so agrees, a plaintiff does not assume a risk of harm arising from the defendant's conduct unless he then knows of the existence of the risk and appreciates its unreasonable character.

# Basketball On Ice

## Situation

On November 28, 2001, the University of Virginia basketball team squared off against Michigan State University at the Richmond (Virginia) Coliseum. The game featured two collegiate powerhouses; Virginia was ranked ninth in the nation and Michigan State was ranked twenty-second. The game was being televised to a nationwide audience on the ESPN Sports Network. With 15:04 left in the second half and Virginia leading the Spartans 31-28, however, officials canceled the game because of unplayable court conditions. The court had become dangerously slick due to a layer of condensation that had formed on the floor. "It was like a roller derby. It was amazing that somebody didn't get seriously hurt," Virginia coach Pete Gillen said after the game.

The Coliseum was to be the site of a professional hockey game two days after the basketball contest. Removing the ice before the basketball game and putting in new ice was not possible. It would have taken at least two full days to make a new ice surface suitable for hockey. So the Coliseum crew laid the basketball court on top of the ice, with a thin barrier separating the ice and the hardwood court. Under ideal conditions, the ice would not have affected the basketball game. Unfortunately, the weather in the days leading up to the basketball game was far from ideal. At tip-off, the temperature outside the arena was 65 degrees, and the ice was melting. Coliseum officials ran the air conditioning units at full blast and turned on all of the available electric fans. Their efforts proved futile, however, leaving the basketball court wet and treacherous.

During the first half of the basketball game, at least six players slipped on the court. In the second half, Virginia center Travis Watson slipped while attempting to cover a Michigan State player on an inbounds play. That was enough for the referees. They immediately stopped the game, prompting a chorus of boos from the fans, some of whom threw beverage bottles onto the floor. One player, Michigan State forward Alan Anderson, was injured in action during the game, suffering a pulled groin muscle.

## Issues

If Alan Anderson or any other player had been seriously injured as a result of the conditions, would the Coliseum officials have been liable in tort?

If players, spectators, or officials had suffered injuries from the bottles thrown by the unruly fans, would the Coliseum officials have been liable in tort?

## Analysis

If there had been serious injuries during the game, the legal analysis would have focused on whether the players assumed the risk of injury. A court would have examined the situation to determine whether it was distinguishable from more typical assumption of risk cases such as *Maddox v. City of New York*. Several distinctions were relevant. For one, officials at the Richmond Coliseum had complete discretion regarding preparations for the basketball game. It was their decision to lay the basketball court on top of the ice. In contrast, when Elliott Maddox was injured at Shea Stadium, stadium officials had no control over the amount of rain that fell before the game. Additionally, Maddox was well aware of the danger posed by the standing water in the outfield and, after assessing that danger, chose to play. The danger posed by the condensation at the Coliseum came from a source—the hockey rink—that was neither obvious nor within view of the players. Therefore, with regard to assessing the danger, the basketball players were in a position that was decidedly inferior to the perspective available to Elliott Maddox at Shea Stadium.

Section 496 D of the Restatement of Torts makes it clear that the Michigan State and Virginia players could not have assumed the risk of playing at the Coliseum unless they understood the risk they were taking and appreciated the unreasonable character and danger posed by playing on top of the ice hockey surface.

Under § 284 of the Restatement of Torts, if Coliseum officials ignored the throwing of beverage bottles and failed to take steps to protect referees, players, and fans, the Coliseum could have been held liable for harm caused by the projectiles. However, it would be unreasonable to expect Coliseum officials to anticipate that cancellation of the game would prompt fans to throw beverage bottles. For purposes of § 435(2) of the Restatement, the throwing of bottles would be a highly extraordinary event. Under § 344, the Coliseum and its officials would not be under a duty to protect others from the bottles until they knew or had reason to know that the fans were throwing the bottles. It is unlikely that any prior experience would have led Coliseum officials to suspect that cancellation of a game would provoke the fans to throw bottles. For this reason, a court would be hard pressed to find that the Coliseum was legally responsible for any harm to persons who might have been hit by the bottles. The result would be in distinct contrast to the duty of stadium officials at a collegiate powerhouse whose teams regularly win championships in football and whose fans routinely tear down the goalposts after each title-clinching game. In that instance, the stadium officials would seem to have a duty, under § 344, to control boisterous fans and protect third parties from injuries that might be caused when fans dismantle the goalposts.

---

## Source

Jeremy Redmon, "Mayor Says City Should Refund Ticket Costs for Slippery Show," *Richmond Times-Dispatch*, 30 November 2001, A1.

## References

RESTATEMENT (SECOND) OF TORTS §§ 284, 344, 435, 496 A, 496 D (1965).

### § 284. Negligent Conduct; Act or Failure to Act

Negligent conduct may be either:

(a) an act which the actor as a reasonable man should recognize as involving an unreasonable risk of causing an invasion of an interest of another, or

(b) a failure to do an act which is necessary for the protection or assistance of another and which the actor is under a duty to do.

### § 344. Business Premises Open to Public: Acts of Third Persons or Animals

A possessor of land who holds it open to the public for entry for his business purposes is subject to liability to members of the public while they are upon the land for such a purpose, for physical harm caused by the accidental, negligent, or intentionally harmful acts of third persons or animals, and by the failure of the possessor to exercise reasonable care to:

(a) discover that such acts are being done or are likely to be done, or

(b) give a warning adequate to enable the visitors to avoid the harm, or otherwise to protect them against it.

### § 435. Foreseeability of Harm or Manner of its Occurrence

(1) If the actor's conduct is a substantial factor in bringing about harm to another, the fact that the actor neither foresaw nor should have foreseen the extent of the harm or the manner in which it occurred does not prevent him from being liable.

(2) The actor's conduct may be held not to be a legal cause of harm to another where after the event and looking back from the harm to the actor's negligent conduct, it

appears to the court highly extraordinary that it should have brought about the harm.

## § 496 A. General Principle [of Assumption of Risk]

A plaintiff who voluntarily assumes a risk of harm arising from the negligent or reckless conduct of the defendant cannot recover for such harm.

## § 496 D. Knowledge and Appreciation of Risk

Except where he expressly so agrees, a plaintiff does not assume a risk of harm arising from the defendant's conduct unless he then knows of the existence of the risk and appreciates its unreasonable character.

# *Duty of Care*

## Special Effects Snafu

### Situation

During the middle of a Montreal Expos game at Olympic Stadium on April 29, 2001, smoke began billowing out from a spot behind the stadium's right field fence, causing alarm to stadium officials and fans alike. Upon investigation, the smoke was found to be coming from an area in the bowels of the stadium that was rented to a Canadian movie company. The movie company had stored a smoke-making machine and other special effects equipment in the rented area. At the time of the incident, the movie company was attempting to test the smoke-making machine.

### Issues

Did the movie company breach its duty of care by testing the smoke-making machine during the game?

In the event that stadium security guards had found it necessary to disable the smoke-making machine and, in doing so, damaged the machine, would they have been liable for a trespass to chattel?

### Analysis

Fortunately, the fans in attendance at Olympic Stadium did not panic at the sight of the smoke and no one was hurt. However, the movie company should have known that operation of the smoke-making machine had the potential for alarming spectators and players at the Stadium. Under § 284 of the Restatement of Torts, the movie company was responsible for recognizing that its actions presented an unreasonable risk to those in attendance at the game. Under § 281 of the Restatement, the movie company would have been liable in tort if the incident had resulted in injuries to others.

If security guards had attempted to shut off the smoke-making machine and, in the process, caused damage to the machine, their actions would have been privileged under § 264 of the Restatement.

## Source

"Hey, We're Playing a Ballgame Here," *USA Today Baseball Weekly*, 25 April-1 May 2001, 3.

## References

RESTATEMENT (SECOND) OF TORTS §§ 264, 281, 282, 283, 284, 289, 302, 435 (1965).

### § 264. Abatement of Nuisance

(1)  One is privileged to commit an act which would otherwise be a trespass to the chattel of another or a conversion of it, for the purpose of abating a private nuisance created or maintained by the other, if the act is a reasonable means of abating the nuisance, and if the other upon demand has failed to abate the nuisance, or the actor reasonably believes that such demand is impractical or useless.

(2)  One to whom a public nuisance causes or threatens special harm is privileged to abate it under the conditions stated in Subsection (1).

### § 281. Statement of the Elements of a Cause of Action for Negligence

The actor is liable for an invasion of an interest of another, if:

(a)  the interest invaded is protected against unintentional invasion, and

(b)  the conduct of the actor is negligent with respect to the other, or a class of persons within which he is included, and

(c)  the actor's conduct is a legal cause of the invasion, and

(d)  the other has not so conducted himself as to disable himself from bringing an action for such invasion.

### § 282. Negligence Defined

In the Restatement of this Subject, negligence is conduct which falls below the standard established by law for the protection of others against unreasonable risk of harm. It does not include conduct recklessly disregardful of an interest of others.

### § 283. Conduct of a Reasonable Man: The Standard

Unless the actor is a child, the standard of conduct to which he must conform to avoid being negligent is that of a reasonable man under like circumstances.

### § 284. Negligent Conduct; Act or Failure to Act

Negligent conduct may be either:

(a) an act which the actor as a reasonable man should recognize as involving an unreasonable risk of causing an invasion of an interest of another, or

(b) a failure to do an act which is necessary for the protection or assistance of another and which the actor is under a duty to do.

### § 289. Recognizing Existence of Risk

The actor is required to recognize that his conduct involves a risk of causing an invasion of another's interest if a reasonable man would do so while exercising:

(a) such attention, perception of the circumstances, memory, knowledge of other pertinent matters, intelligence, and judgment as a reasonable man would have; and

(b) such superior attention, perception, memory, knowledge, intelligence, and judgment as the actor himself has.

### § 302. Risk of Direct or Indirect Harm

A negligent act or omission may be one which involves an unreasonable risk of harm to another through either:

(a) the continuous operation of a force started or continued by the act or omission, or

(b) the foreseeable action of the other, a third person, an animal, or a force of nature.

### § 435. Foreseeability of Harm or Manner of its Occurrence

(1) If the actor's conduct is a substantial factor in bringing about harm to another, the fact that the actor neither foresaw nor should have foreseen the extent of the harm or the manner in which it occurred does not prevent him from being liable.

(2) The actor's conduct may be held not to be a legal cause of harm to another where after the event and looking back from the harm to the actor's negligent conduct, it appears to the court highly extraordinary that it should have brought about the harm.

# Yankee Stadium "Death Seat"

## Situation

On April 13, 1998, a 500-pound concrete and steel beam forming part of the upper deck at Yankee Stadium fell just as the New York Yankees and California Angels were about to begin batting practice in preparation for a twilight game. The beam landed atop Seat 7 in the second row of Section 22. When reporting the incident, newspapers referred to Seat 7 as the "Death Seat." No less an authority than New York Mayor Rudolph Giuliani commented, "You could see that if someone were sitting there at the time that the beam came down, that person would be dead."

## Issue

If an individual had been occupying Seat 7 when the concrete and steel beam fell, would the New York Yankees have been liable?

## Analysis

The Yankees lease Yankee Stadium from the city of New York. The lease arrangement states that the Yankees are responsible for maintenance of the Stadium. The city of New York and the Yankees are jointly responsible for protecting spectators from injuries due to structural defects. If the falling beam had caused harm to an occupant of Seat 7, both the Yankees and the city would have shared liability.

Under § 328 A of the Restatement of Torts, to establish liability on the part of the Yankees and the city, a plaintiff would have had to prove four elements: (1) there was a duty to protect the occupant of Seat 7 from harm; (2) there was a breach of that duty; (3) there was actual injury, loss or damages; and (4) the failure to protect against structural defects was the cause of the injury, loss or damages.

---

## Sources

Randy Kennedy, "Yankee Stadium Closed as Beam Falls onto Seats," *The N.Y. Times*, 14 April 1998, A1.

Blaine Harden, "Letter from New York: One Steel Beam May Not Be Enough to Wreck the House That Ruth Built," *The N.Y. Times*, 16 April 1998, A2.

## References

Restatement (Second) of Torts §§ 281, 328 A, 328 D (1965).

### § 281. Statement of the Elements of a Cause of Action for Negligence

The actor is liable for an invasion of an interest of another, if:

(a) the interest invaded is protected against unintentional invasion, and

(b) the conduct of the actor is negligent with respect to the other, or a class of persons within which he is included, and

(c) the actor's conduct is a legal cause of the invasion, and

(d) the other has not so conducted himself as to disable himself from bringing an action for such invasion.

### § 328 A. Burden of Proof

In an action for negligence the plaintiff has the burden of proving:

(a) facts which give rise to a legal duty on the part of the defendant to conform to the standard of conduct established by law for the protection of the plaintiff,

(b) failure of the defendant to conform to the standard of conduct,

(c) that such failure is a legal cause of the harm suffered by the plaintiff, and

(d) that the plaintiff has in fact suffered harm of a kind legally compensable by damages.

### § 328 D. Res Ipsa Loquitur

(1) It may be inferred that harm suffered by the plaintiff is caused by negligence of the defendant when:

(a) the event is of a kind which ordinarily does not occur in the absence of negligence;

(b) other responsible causes, including the conduct of the plaintiff and third persons, are sufficiently eliminated by the evidence; and

(c) the indicated negligence is within the scope of the defendant's duty to the plaintiff.

(2) It is the function of the court to determine whether the inference may reasonably be drawn by the jury, or whether it must necessarily be drawn.

(3) It is the function of the jury to determine whether the inference is to be drawn in any case where different conclusions may reasonably be reached.

# Robbery On The 13th Fairway

## Situation

Golfer Michael Dudas was playing the thirteenth hole at Glenwood Golf Club in Richmond, Virginia when he was accosted by two unknown male trespassers. The trespassers pulled a gun, took Dudas's money and shot him in the leg. The golfer sued the golf club for $2,350,000. He argued that the golf club had an obligation to protect him from criminal acts committed by others. Dudas uncovered evidence showing that, in the month before he was robbed, there had been two armed robberies and one attempted robbery on the golf course. One of the earlier robberies had also taken place on the thirteenth hole. Prior to those two armed robberies and one attempted robbery, the last such criminal activity on the course had occurred seventeen months earlier.

## Issue

Under the law of torts, did the Glenwood Golf Club have a duty to warn its patrons that they might encounter criminal behavior while playing the course?

## Analysis

Under § 344 of the Restatement of Torts, a business that opens its land to the public for entry is not an absolute insurer of the safety of visitors against the acts of others. At the same time, however, the business is under a duty to exercise reasonable care to protect visitors. In *Dudas v. Glenwood Golf Club, Inc.*, the court attempted to balance the difficulty of providing meaningful security in the unique environment of a golf course against the risk of criminal activity. The court concluded that a golf course is not under an absolute duty to protect its visitors from assaults by unknown third parties. In the court's view, based on the relatively low level of criminal activity at the Glenwood Golf Club, golfers were not in "imminent danger" of criminal assault. The court ruled, therefore, that the golf course was not under a duty to warn visitors of the potential danger of criminal assaults by third parties.

## Source

*Dudas v. Glenwood Golf Club, Inc.*, 261 Va. 133, 540 S.E.2d 129 (2001).

## Reference

RESTATEMENT (SECOND) OF TORTS § 344 (1965).

### § 344. Business Premises Open to Public: Acts of Third Persons or Animals

A possessor of land who holds it open to the public for entry for his business purposes is subject to liability to members of the public while they are upon the land for such a purpose, for physical harm caused by the accidental, negligent, or intentionally harmful acts of third persons or animals, and by the failure of the possessor to exercise reasonable care to:

(a) discover that such acts are being done or are likely to be done, or

(b) give a warning adequate to enable the visitors to avoid the harm, or otherwise to protect them against it.

# Legal Cause of Injury

## Proximate Dog, Remote Cause

### Situation

Early in his coaching career, George Mason University basketball coach Jim Larranaga was an assistant coach at the University of Virginia. Larranaga once traveled to upstate New York to recruit high school basketball star Tom Sheehey for the Cavaliers. Larranaga flew in a Lear jet to meet Sheehey at his home. Sheehey was to accompany Larranaga back to Virginia for a campus visit. After arriving at an airport near Sheehey's home, Larranaga took a taxi to the Sheehey residence. Larranaga and Sheehey exchanged pleasantries, and the two got into the taxi to go back to the airport. When the cab driver put the taxi into gear, Sheehey's dog ran in pursuit. The taxi hit the dog. Larranaga and Sheehey quickly hopped from the cab. In an effort to comfort his pet, Sheehey picked the dog up in his arms. In distress, the dog bit Sheehey, inflicting a wound.

### Issue

Assuming that the taxi driver was negligent in driving his taxi and that, as a result of his negligence, he hit Tom Sheehey's dog, would the taxi driver have been liable to Sheehey for his wound?

### Analysis

The essential question would be whether the taxi driver's negligence was a legal cause of the injury to Sheehey. Section 431 of the Restatement asks, first, whether the cabbie's driving was a substantial factor in the injury to Sheehey. Once it was established that the taxi driver's negligence was a substantial factor in causing the harm, § 431 would look to see if there was a rule of law relieving the taxi driver from liability. One such rule of law, referenced in § 435(2), is the doctrine of foreseeability. Under § 435(2), looking back from the injury to the taxi driver's negligence, it would be highly extraordinary that the negligence would result in Sheehey suffering a dog bite. In the words of Justice Cardozo, the dog bite would not have been within the "range of apprehension." The injury to the dog was a proximate result of the taxi driver's act of driving. The injury to Sheehey was considerably more remote—and not foreseeable.

## References

RESTATEMENT (SECOND) OF TORTS §§ 8, 8 A, 281, 282, 430, 431, 435 (1965).

### § 8. Unavoidable Accident

The words "unavoidable accident" are used throughout the Restatement of this Subject to denote the fact that the harm which is so described is not caused by any tortious act of the one whose conduct is in question.

### § 8 A. Intent

The word "intent" is used throughout the Restatement of this Subject to denote the fact that the actor desires to cause consequences of his act, or that he believes that the consequences are substantially certain to result from it.

### § 281. Statement of the Elements of a Cause of Action for Negligence

The actor is liable for an invasion of an interest of another, if:

(a)   the interest invaded is protected against unintentional invasion, and

(b)   the conduct of the actor is negligent with respect to the other, or a class of persons within which he is included, and

(c)   the actor's conduct is a legal cause of the invasion, and

(d)   the other has not so conducted himself as to disable himself from bringing an action for such invasion.

### § 282. Negligence Defined

In the Restatement of this Subject, negligence is conduct which falls below the standard established by law for the protection of others against unreasonable risk of harm. It does not include conduct recklessly disregardful of an interest of others.

### § 430. Necessity of Adequate Causal Relation

In order that a negligent actor shall be liable for another's harm, it is necessary not only that the actor's conduct be negligent toward the other, but also that the negligence of the actor be a legal cause of the other's harm.

### § 431. What Constitutes Legal Cause

The actor's negligent conduct is a legal cause of harm to another if:

(a)   his conduct is a substantial factor in bringing about the harm, and

(b) there is no rule of law relieving the actor from liability because of the manner in which his negligence has resulted in the harm.

## § 435. Foreseeability of Harm or Manner of its Occurrence

(1) If the actor's conduct is a substantial factor in bringing about harm to another, the fact that the actor neither foresaw nor should have foreseen the extent of the harm or the manner in which it occurred does not prevent him from being liable.

(2) The actor's conduct may be held not to be a legal cause of harm to another where after the event and looking back from the harm to the actor's negligent conduct, it appears to the court highly extraordinary that it should have brought about the harm.

# Lousy Food, Lousy Foot

## Situation

The men's basketball team of St. John's University competed in the 1999 National Collegiate Athletic Association basketball tournament. Two days before St. John's was to play the University of Maryland, the Red Storm's guard and leading scorer, Ron Artest, became sick to his stomach. While staying with his teammates at a Knoxville, Tennessee hotel, Artest ate some food that did not agree with him. Afterwards, while resting in his hotel room, Artest made a hurried trip to the bathroom to throw up. In his haste, Artest banged his right foot against the bottom of his bed—leaving him with both an upset stomach and an injured foot. "I ate some lousy food," Artest said. "It was bad, and my foot hurt after that. But I'm 99.9 percent sure it will be okay." In the game against Maryland, Artest did not have one of his better performances, scoring only 8 points in 39 minutes of action.

## Issue

Under the law of torts, would the restaurant that served Artest "lousy food" be liable for the injury to his foot?

## Analysis

What is clear is that the restaurant had an obligation to serve Artest something other than "lousy food." The restaurant or its food suppliers may have been liable for the bad food and for making Artest sick. The illness was a proximate result of the bad food. However, as with the dog bite suffered by Tom Sheehey, § 435 of the Restatement of Torts is relevant. Looking back from Artest's injury to the source of the lousy food, it would be highly extraordinary that the bad food should have brought about the harm to Artest's foot. Even if Artest's injured foot contributed to his low point total, neither the injury nor his sub-par scoring against Maryland was foreseeable. The bad food was not a legal cause of either.

## Source

C. Jemal Horton and Neil H. Greenberger, "Gators' Shannon Has Ticket to Final Four," *The Washington Post*, 18 March 1999, D6.

# References

RESTATEMENT (SECOND) OF TORTS §§ 8, 8 A, 281, 282, 430, 431, 435 (1965).

### § 8. Unavoidable Accident

The words "unavoidable accident" are used throughout the Restatement of this Subject to denote the fact that the harm which is so described is not caused by any tortious act of the one whose conduct is in question.

### § 8 A. Intent

The word "intent" is used throughout the Restatement of this Subject to denote the fact that the actor desires to cause consequences of his act, or that he believes that the consequences are substantially certain to result from it.

### § 281. Statement of the Elements of a Cause of Action for Negligence

The actor is liable for an invasion of an interest of another, if:

(a) the interest invaded is protected against unintentional invasion, and

(b) the conduct of the actor is negligent with respect to the other, or a class of persons within which he is included, and

(c) the actor's conduct is a legal cause of the invasion, and

(d) the other has not so conducted himself as to disable himself from bringing an action for such invasion.

### § 282. Negligence Defined

In the Restatement of this Subject, negligence is conduct which falls below the standard established by law for the protection of others against unreasonable risk of harm. It does not include conduct recklessly disregardful of an interest of others.

### § 430. Necessity of Adequate Causal Relation

In order that a negligent actor shall be liable for another's harm, it is necessary not only that the actor's conduct be negligent toward the other, but also that the negligence of the actor be a legal cause of the other's harm.

### § 431. What Constitutes Legal Cause

The actor's negligent conduct is a legal cause of harm to another if:

(a) his conduct is a substantial factor in bringing about the harm, and

(b) there is no rule of law relieving the actor from liability because of the manner in which his negligence has resulted in the harm.

## § 435. Foreseeability of Harm or Manner of its Occurrence

(1) If the actor's conduct is a substantial factor in bringing about harm to another, the fact that the actor neither foresaw nor should have foreseen the extent of the harm or the manner in which it occurred does not prevent him from being liable.

(2) The actor's conduct may be held not to be a legal cause of harm to another where after the event and looking back from the harm to the actor's negligent conduct, it appears to the court highly extraordinary that it should have brought about the harm.

# Closing Camden Yards

## Situation

When a 60-car freight train derailed and set off a fire inside the Howard Street train tunnel in Baltimore on the afternoon of July 18, 2001, it brought traffic in the vicinity to a standstill. The train had begun its trip in North Carolina and was headed for New Jersey. Nine of the train's cars were carrying hazardous materials, including propylene glycol, which is used in de-icing fluids, and hydrochloric acid.

Police crews closed off all of the major roads into the city while firefighters battled the intense underground fire and suffocating smoke for the better part of five days. The accident caused havoc at neighboring Oriole Park at Camden Yards. The fire started just as the Orioles were preparing for a night game against the Texas Rangers. After the fire broke out, a cloud of thick smoke settled over the ballpark. The Orioles hastily canceled the game. Panicked players sprinted for their cars in full uniform. For three straight days, the Orioles had to cancel their games. City officials, fearing that the combination of fire and hydrochloric acid would produce dangerous vapors, would not allow the Orioles to resume play at Camden Yards until all of the cars carrying hazardous materials were secured and the fire contained. As a result, the Orioles lost two home dates against the Texas Rangers and one against the Anaheim Angels and were deprived of more than $1 million in ticket and concession sales.

The National Transportation Safety Board quickly opened an investigation into the cause of the derailment. However, three years after the accident, NTSB still had not determined the cause. Experts feared that NTSB might never reach a firm conclusion because the fire destroyed much of the evidence that would have been useful. In the aftermath of the accident, there were two prominent theories regarding the cause. Under one theory, there may have been a leak in a water main that ran near the walls of the tunnel, and the leak may have then eroded the soil near the tunnel walls, causing bricks from the walls to fall onto the tracks and leading to the derailment. Under another theory, CSX was negligent in maintaining the tracks, and the faulty condition of the tracks caused the derailment, which, in turn, sparked the fire.

The insurance company for the Orioles sued both CSX, alleging negligent and careless maintenance of the railroad tracks, and the city of Baltimore, alleging negligent and careless maintenance of the municipal water system.

## Issue

Under the law of torts, would CSX and/or the city of Baltimore be liable to the Orioles for the ticket and concession sales lost as a result of cancellation of the three home games?

## Analysis

The threat of dangerous vapors at Camden Yards was the product of three separate circumstances: (1) the presence of chemicals on the train, (2) the derailment, and (3) the outbreak of fire. Without any one of these three circumstances, there would have been no harmful vapors. There is no question that the Orioles suffered harm. The only issue is whether either CSX or the city of Baltimore, or both parties, were liable for the harm.

The law distinguishes between proximate and remote effects. Proximate effects can be anticipated. Remote effects are not foreseeable and, for that reason, cannot be anticipated. Before a court awards monetary compensation for damages, it must find that the conduct of the defendant was the proximate cause of the injury suffered by the plaintiff. Even people who owe a duty of care to others cannot be held liable for consequences of their acts that are too remote and therefore not foreseeable. The distinction between proximate and remote results becomes particularly significant in a situation such as the Howard Street tunnel accident.

Justice Cardozo would impose liability only if the damages suffered by the Orioles were within the range of apprehension. The Restatement of Torts would look at the issue differently. Under § 435 of the Restatement, the fact that neither CSX nor the city of Baltimore could have foreseen the extent of the harm or the manner in which it occurred would not prevent either party from being liable. Section 433 of the Restatement would ask whether the conduct by either CSX or the city of Baltimore created a force or series of forces which were in continuous and active operation up to the time of the harm. Under § 432 of the Restatement, if negligence on the part of the city of Baltimore and negligence by CSX actively contributed to the accident and each force was sufficient to bring about the harm to the Orioles, negligence attributed to both CSX and the city could each be found to be a substantial factor in causing the harm.

## Sources

Tom Ramstack, "Pipe Leak, Erosion Eyed in Derailing; Baltimore Denies Role in Train Wreck," *The Washington Times*, 2 July 2003, C8.

Laura Vozzella, "City to File Suit Against CSX in '01 Derailment; Action Claims the Railroad Is Responsible for Accident," *The Baltimore Sun*, 16 July 2004, 1B.

## References

*Palsgraf v. Long Island Railroad Co.*, 248 N.Y. 339, 162 N.E. 99 (1928).

RESTATEMENT (SECOND) OF TORTS §§ 328 D, 432, 433, 433 A, 435 (1965).

### § 328 D. Res Ipsa Loquitur

(1) It may be inferred that harm suffered by the plaintiff is caused by negligence of the defendant when:

    (a) the event is of a kind which ordinarily does not occur in the absence of negligence;

    (b) other responsible causes, including the conduct of the plaintiff and third persons, are sufficiently eliminated by the evidence; and

    (c) the indicated negligence is within the scope of the defendant's duty to the plaintiff.

(2) It is the function of the court to determine whether the inference may reasonably be drawn by the jury, or whether it must necessarily be drawn.

(3) It is the function of the jury to determine whether the inference is to be drawn in any case where different conclusions may reasonably be reached.

### § 432. Negligent Conduct as Necessary Antecedent of Harm

(1) Except as stated in Subsection (2), the actor's negligent conduct is not a substantial factor in bringing about harm to another if the harm would have been sustained even if the actor had not been negligent.

(2) If two forces are actively operating, one because of the actor's negligence, the other not because of any misconduct on his part, and each of itself is sufficient to bring about harm to another, the actor's negligence may be found to be a substantial factor in bringing it about.

### § 433. Considerations Important in Determining Whether Negligent Conduct is Substantial Factor in Producing Harm

The following considerations are in themselves or in combination with one another important in determining whether the actor's conduct is a substantial factor in bringing about harm to another:

(a) the number of other factors which contribute in producing the harm and the extent of the effect which they have in producing it;

(b) whether the actor's conduct has created a force or series of forces which are in continuous and active operation up to the time of the harm, or has created a situation harmless unless acted upon by other forces for which the actor is not responsible;

(c) lapse of time.

### § 433 A. Apportionment of Harm to Causes

(1) Damages for harm are to be apportioned among two or more causes where:

(a) there are distinct harms, or

(b) there is a reasonable basis for determining the contribution of each cause to a single harm.

(2) Damages for any other harm cannot be apportioned among two or more causes.

### § 435. Foreseeability of Harm or Manner of its Occurrence

(1) If the actor's conduct is a substantial factor in bringing about harm to another, the fact that the actor neither foresaw nor should have foreseen the extent of the harm or the manner in which it occurred does not prevent him from being liable.

(2) The actor's conduct may be held not to be a legal cause of harm to another where after the event and looking back from the harm to the actor's negligent conduct, it appears to the court highly extraordinary that it should have brought about the harm.

# Woe Is Van Gundy

## Situation

On the evening of Wednesday, May 17, 2000, New York Knicks coach Jeff Van Gundy had a lot on his mind. His team had just delivered a woeful performance in Miami during the fifth game of the Eastern Conference Semifinals against the Miami Heat. Center Patrick Ewing's knees were showing their age, forward Marcus Camby was playing passively, and guards Chris Childs and Charlie Ward were lofting up shots that were beyond their customary range. To top it all off, Van Gundy's car, a 1995 Honda Civic, was destroyed in a freak occurrence at Westchester County Airport just after the Knicks' chartered aircraft landed upon its return from Miami. According to eyewitnesses, as the team's plane taxied to an area near where the players and staff had parked their vehicles, one of the plane's engines emitted a large amount of thrust. The blast lifted Van Gundy's Honda and tossed it on top of several other cars. No one was hurt in the incident, but forward Allan Houston's Mercedes and two other cars were damaged.

## Issue

Under the law of tort, who would be liable for the destruction of Van Gundy's Honda and the damage to Houston's Mercedes?

## Analysis

Sorting out the liability in this case would be a formidable task for any jurist. Liability could rest with: (a) the airplane manufacturer for a possibly latent defect in the plane's engine; (b) the owner of the aircraft for faulty maintenance; (c) the pilot of the chartered aircraft for improper operation or taxiing too close to the team's parking area; (d) Jeff Van Gundy for parking too close to the area where the airplane would stop; or (e) none of these parties because the damage was the result of an unavoidable accident.

The inquiry under tort law would begin with an assessment of the duty of care owed by each party having potential liability. The airplane manufacturer owed a duty to the operator of the airplane charter and to the Knicks to provide a plane that was fit for safe operation. The charter company owed a duty to its customers to properly maintain the plane. The pilot owed a duty to the Knicks to operate the airplane in a safe manner. Under § 435 of the Restatement of Torts, if the conduct of any of these parties were a substantial factor in causing the accident, the fact that they could not have foreseen the manner in which the harm occurred would not prevent them from being held liable. Under § 433 A of the Restatement, liability for the damages that occurred could be apportioned among two or more causes or parties if there was a reasonable basis for determining the contribution of each cause or party to the harm.

Alternatively, in the event a court could not identify the precise cause of the accident, it might still hold the charter company liable under the doctrine of *res ipsa loquitur* set forth in § 328 D of the Restatement. *Res ipsa loquitur* would come into play if the court determined that the blast from the airplane engine would not ordinarily have occurred unless there had been some form of negligent conduct. If all other possible causes for the accident were ruled out, the court could conclude, under § 328 D, that the responsibility for preventing such accidents was within the scope of the duty that the charter company owed to Jeff Van Gundy and the Knicks.

---

## Source

Mike Wise, *From Team to Car, Woe Is Van Gundy*, THE N.Y. TIMES, May 29, 2000, D3.

## References

RESTATEMENT (SECOND) OF TORTS §§ 281, 328 D, 433, 433 A, 435 (1965).

### § 281. Statement of the Elements of a Cause of Action for Negligence

The actor is liable for an invasion of an interest of another, if:

- (a) the interest invaded is protected against unintentional invasion, and
- (b) the conduct of the actor is negligent with respect to the other, or a class of persons within which he is included, and
- (c) the actor's conduct is a legal cause of the invasion, and
- (d) the other has not so conducted himself as to disable himself from bringing an action for such invasion.

### § 328 D. Res Ipsa Loquitur

(1) It may be inferred that harm suffered by the plaintiff is caused by negligence of the defendant when:

- (a) the event is of a kind which ordinarily does not occur in the absence of negligence;

(b) other responsible causes, including the conduct of the plaintiff and third persons, are sufficiently eliminated by the evidence; and

(c) the indicated negligence is within the scope of the defendant's duty to the plaintiff.

(2) It is the function of the court to determine whether the inference may reasonably be drawn by the jury, or whether it must necessarily be drawn.

(3) It is the function of the jury to determine whether the inference is to be drawn in any case where different conclusions may reasonably be reached.

## § 433. Considerations Important in Determining Whether Negligent Conduct is Substantial Factor in Producing Harm

The following considerations are in themselves or in combination with one another important in determining whether the actor's conduct is a substantial factor in bringing about harm to another:

(a) the number of other factors which contribute in producing the harm and the extent of the effect which they have in producing it;

(b) whether the actor's conduct has created a force or series of forces which are in continuous and active operation up to the time of the harm, or has created a situation harmless unless acted upon by other forces for which the actor is not responsible;

(c) lapse of time.

## § 433 A. Apportionment of Harm to Causes

(1) Damages for harm are to be apportioned among two or more causes where:

(a) there are distinct harms, or

(b) there is a reasonable basis for determining the contribution of each cause to a single harm.

(2) Damages for any other harm cannot be apportioned among two or more causes.

## § 435. Foreseeability of Harm or Manner of its Occurrence

(1) If the actor's conduct is a substantial factor in bringing about harm to another, the fact that the actor neither foresaw nor should have foreseen the extent of the harm or the manner in which it occurred does not prevent him from being liable.

(2) The actor's conduct may be held not to be a legal cause of harm to another where after the event and looking back from the harm to the actor's negligent conduct, it

appears to the court highly extraordinary that it should have brought about the harm.

# A Picture Worth $735,000

## Situation

A picture of current Texas Rangers pitcher R.A. Dickey appeared on the cover of *Baseball America*'s 1996 Olympic Preview. At the time, Dickey was a key member of the U.S. Olympic team's starting rotation. The picture portrayed Dickey with four other U.S. Olympic pitchers above a caption that read, "Armed For Battle." Weeks before the Olympic Preview issue hit the streets, the Texas Rangers had taken Dickey in the first round of the amateur draft and had offered him a bonus of $810,000 to sign with the organization. The offer was still on the table when a doctor employed by the Rangers came across the Olympic Preview cover photo. From the doctor's perspective, Dickey's right arm seemed to be hanging in an awkward position. Fearing a problem with the pitcher's arm, the doctor advised the Rangers to have Dickey undergo a physical before agreeing to terms on his contract. The results of the physical were not good. Doctors found that Dickey lacked any semblance of an ulnar collateral ligament in his right arm. The medical consensus was that, without an ulnar collateral ligament, Dickey had little or no chance of a long-term career in baseball. The doctors advised the Rangers that Dickey's arm would not tolerate the rigors of a professional career. The team quickly retracted its $810,000 offer. The Rangers then signed Dickey to a $75,000 bonus, largely as a compassionate gesture.

## Issue

Under the law of torts, would R.A. Dickey have had any legal recourse against *Baseball America* for the untimely photograph that prompted the Rangers to reduce their offer by $735,000?

## Analysis

Traditional tort analysis would begin with the question of whether *Baseball America* owed a duty of care to R.A. Dickey. It seems clear that *Baseball America* did not owe a duty of care to Dickey. The harm was accidental, seemingly unavoidable, and certainly not intentionally caused by *Baseball America*. Section 8 A of the Restatement of Torts states that intent exists when an actor desires to cause the consequences of his act or believes that the consequences are substantially certain to result from it. Clearly, there was no intent by *Baseball America* to deprive Dickey of the $810,000 bonus. Moreover, under § 435 of the Restatement, looking back from the harm to the actions of *Baseball America*, it would have been highly extraordinary that placing a picture of Dickey on the cover of the Olympic Preview issue should have brought about financial harm.

There was no indication that Dickey held *Baseball America* responsible for the loss of the $810,000 signing bonus. In any event, neither the photograph nor Dickey's lack of an ulnar collateral ligament seemed to derail his baseball career. He enjoyed a highly successful season with the Triple-A Oklahoma RedHawks in 2001 and late that season, at age 26, he made his major league debut with the Texas Rangers. After spending the 2002 season back with Oklahoma, Dickey was promoted to Texas early in 2003 and posted a 9-8 won-lost record in 38 appearances with the Rangers. During 2004, he appeared in 25 games for the Rangers, winning 6 and losing 7.

---

## Source

Alan Schwarz, "Rangers' Dickey Defies Odds As Often As Possible," *Baseball America*, 22 June 2003, 9.

## References

RESTATEMENT (SECOND) OF TORTS §§ 8, 8 A, 435 (1965).

### § 8. Unavoidable Accident

The words "unavoidable accident" are used throughout the Restatement of this Subject to denote the fact that the harm which is so described is not caused by any tortious act of the one whose conduct is in question.

### § 8 A. Intent

The word "intent" is used throughout the Restatement of this Subject to denote the fact that the actor desires to cause consequences of his act, or that he believes that the consequences are substantially certain to result from it.

### § 435. Foreseeability of Harm or Manner of its Occurrence

(1) If the actor's conduct is a substantial factor in bringing about harm to another, the fact that the actor neither foresaw nor should have foreseen the extent of the harm or the manner in which it occurred does not prevent him from being liable.

(2) The actor's conduct may be held not to be a legal cause of harm to another where after the event and looking back from the harm to the actor's negligent conduct, it

appears to the court highly extraordinary that it should have brought about the harm.

# Section 2:

# **Contract Cases**

# The Offer

## A Desperate Offer

### Situation

On November 6, 2000, less than a week into the 2000-2001 NBA season, Paul Westphal, then the coach of the Seattle SuperSonics basketball team, met with the players on his team and offered to resign. It was an act of desperation on Westphal's part. He was frustrated by bickering and insubordination among the players and his inability to mold the team into a cohesive unit.

### Issue

Did Westphal's offer to resign form the basis for a valid contract?

### Analysis

Under § 71(3) of the Restatement of Contracts, the destruction of a legal relationship can form the consideration for a contract. If Westphal had any intention of quitting, however, he was directing his offer to the wrong audience. The only person with the power of acceptance, as that term is used in § 29(1) of the Restatement, was SuperSonics owner Barry Ackerly. With respect to Westphal's contractual undertaking as coach of the team, the Sonics players were neither **promisors** nor **promisees**. If and when Westphal worked out a termination agreement with the team's management, the players would have been no more than incidental beneficiaries. Therefore, even if the players had "accepted" Westphal's offer, Westphal would not have been obligated to resign. His offer did not form the basis for a valid contract. (With the team in turmoil, Westphal did not last through the end of the month. The Sonics fired him on November 27th.)

---

### Source

"Westphal Offered to Quit," *The Washington Post*, 18 November 2000, D2.

### References

RESTATEMENT (SECOND) OF CONTRACTS §§ 1, 20, 29, 71, 315 (1981).

### § 1. Contract Defined

A contract is a promise or a set of promises for the breach of which the law gives a remedy, or the performance of which the law in some way recognizes as a duty.

### § 20. Effect of Misunderstanding

(1) There is no manifestation of mutual assent to an exchange if the parties attach materially different meanings to their manifestations and (a) neither party knows or has reason to know the meaning attached by the other; or (b) each party knows or each party has reason to know the meaning attached by the other.

(2) The manifestations of the parties are operative in accordance with the meaning attached to them by one of the parties if (a) that party does not know of any different meaning attached by the other; and the other knows the meaning attached by the first party; or (b) that party has no reason to know of any different meaning attached by the other, and the other has reason to know the meaning attached by the first party.

### § 29. To Whom an Offer is Addressed

(1) The manifested intention of the offeror determines the person or persons in whom is created a power of acceptance.

(2) An offer may create a power of acceptance in a specified person or in one or more of a specified group or class of persons, acting separately or together, or in anyone or everyone who makes a specified promise or renders a specified performance.

### § 71. Requirement of Exchange; Types of Exchange

(1) To constitute consideration, a performance or a return promise must be bargained for.

(2) A performance or return promise is bargained for if it is sought by the promisor in exchange for his promise and is given by the promisee in exchange for that promise.

(3) The performance may consist of

    (a) an act other than a promise, or

    (b) a forbearance, or

    (c) the creation, modification, or destruction of a legal relation.

(4) The performance or return promise may be given to the promisor or to some other person. It may be given by the promisee or by some other person.

## § 315. Effect of a Promise of Incidental Benefit

An incidental beneficiary acquires by virtue of the promise no right against the promisor or the promisee.

# The Billboard Offer

## Situation

During the National Basketball Association's 2000-2001 season, there was rampant speculation as to where Sacramento Kings all-star forward Chris Webber would be playing when the NBA opened its doors the following season. After playing for three years in Sacramento, Webber was due to become a free agent in the spring of 2001. There were reports that he wanted to join Michael Jordan and the Washington Wizards. Other reports had Webber, a frequent visitor to Los Angeles, ready to sign with the Lakers. Sacramento, a city that Webber found "lacking in a lot of diversity," seemed not to be high on his list of possible cities. The Kings' owners, Gavin and Joe Maloof, knew that it would take more than their millions of dollars to entice Webber to stay. They appealed to Webber with a billboard message positioned alongside Interstate 80, not far from the team's Arco Arena. The billboard pictured Joe Maloof riding a lawn mower while Gavin extended a promise in extra large letters to Webber: "Chris, Joe will mow your lawn if you stay."

## Issue

Under the law of contracts, did the Maloofs' billboard message constitute a valid offer to Webber?

## Analysis

There is little doubt that the Maloofs were joking, but the literal words on the billboard presented the appearance of a bona fide offer. In any event, few NBA insiders gave the Kings any reasonable chance of resigning Webber. Joke or no joke, Joe Maloof probably gave little thought to ever having to mow Webber's lawn. On July 21, 2001, the "offer" became more than a moot point when Webber signed a seven-year, $122.7 million contract to stay with the Kings. "I looked at all my options," Webber told the press, "and after all the pluses and minuses, there was nothing better than being here." The comment to § 18 of the Restatement of Contracts discusses offers made in jest. According to the Restatement, if all the parties to what would otherwise be a bargain display an intention not to take the transaction seriously, the requirement for valid assent to the exchange has not been satisfied. In some cases, the setting makes it clear that there is no contract, as when a business transaction is simulated on a stage during a dramatic performance or when a basketball team posts an offer to one of its players on a highway billboard.

## Source

"Webber Gets a Kings' Ransom: Seven-Year, $122.7 Million Deal," *The Washington Post*, 22 July 2001, D7.

## References

RESTATEMENT (SECOND) OF CONTRACTS §§ 18, 24, 26, 29, 209 (1981).

### § 18. Manifestation of Mutual Assent

Manifestation of mutual assent to an exchange requires that each party either make a promise or begin or render a performance.

### § 24. Offer Defined

An offer is the manifestation of willingness to enter into a bargain, so made as to justify another person in understanding that his assent to that bargain is invited and will conclude it.

### § 26. Preliminary Negotiations

A manifestation of willingness to enter into a bargain is not an offer if the person to whom it is addressed knows or has reason to know that the person making it does not intend to conclude a bargain until he has made a further manifestation of assent.

### § 29. To Whom an Offer is Addressed

(1) The manifested intention of the offeror determines the person or persons in whom is created a power of acceptance.

(2) An offer may create a power of acceptance in a specified person or in one or more of a specified group or class of persons, acting separately or together, or in anyone or everyone who makes a specified promise or renders a specified performance.

### § 209. Integrated Agreements

(1) An integrated agreement is a writing or writings constituting a final expression of one or more terms of an agreement.

(2) Whether there is an integrated agreement is to be determined by the court as a question preliminary to determination of a question of interpretation or to application of the parol evidence rule.

(3) Where the parties reduce an agreement to a writing which in view of its completeness and specificity reasonably appears to be a complete agreement, it is taken to be an integrated agreement unless it is established by other evidence that the writing did not constitute a final expression.

# This For Real?

## Situation

On June 20, 2000, the Vancouver [now Memphis] Grizzlies of the National Basketball Association worked out rookie guard prospects Speedy Claxton of Hofstra and Eddie Gill of Weber State. The Grizzlies had the good fortune of picking second in the year 2000 draft of collegiate and high school players. At the workout, Grizzlies player personnel director Tony Barone told Claxton and Gill, "I'm empowered to say that if you make a shot from center court, you'll be the Number 2 pick in the draft."

## Issue

Assuming that either Speedy Claxton or Eddie Gill made the shot from center court, thereby extending the performance that Barone required, were the Vancouver Grizzlies obligated to select the player with the Number 2 pick?

## Analysis

As player personnel director, Barone really was empowered to make such a commitment, so his statement was cloaked with some credibility. "This for real?" Claxton asked. Barone nodded. Claxton then stepped up to center court and sank his shot. Gill followed, and he hit his shot as well. On one level, the incident reflects a classic case of offer and acceptance. Barone extended the offer, telling both players what they had to do to be selected as the Number 2 pick in the draft. Both players responded to Barone's offer and satisfied the condition. Each "accepted" the offer.

A close look at Barone's "offer" suggests, however, that he really was joking. Clearly, the Grizzlies could only take one player with the Number 2 pick. By dangling the prospect of that single pick, on equal terms, to two different players, Barone was inviting a potentially impossible outcome. Further, Barone's words themselves do not indicate a commitment. He told the players he was "empowered to say" that they would be taken with the Number 2 pick. Declaring that a player would be the Number 2 pick implies a commitment. Being "empowered to say" does not carry the same implication. Barone's words fell short of extending a firm offer. Ultimately the Grizzlies did not make either Claxton or Gill the Number 2 pick in the draft. That distinction went to Stromile Swift, a 6'9" guard-forward from Louisiana State University.

Nonetheless, Barone would do well to be more circumspect with his words. The comments to § 18 of the Restatement of Contracts make it clear that, while the law allows some latitude for jokes, the joker must be careful. If all parties recognize that an offer is extended in jest, there is no power of acceptance. However, if one party is deceived and has no reason to know of the joke, the law may take the joker at his word. As stated in the case of *Plate v. Durst*, "[j]okes are sometimes taken seriously by the young and inexperienced in the deceptive ways of the business world and if such is the case, and thereby the person deceived is led to give valuable services in the full belief and expectation that the joker is earnest, the law will also take the joker at his word, and give him good reason to smile."

If Barone's words had formed a valid offer, there would have been a ready mechanism under the Restatement for resolving the issue of the "acceptance" by both Claxton and Gill. The comment accompanying § 29 of the Restatement makes it clear that once Claxton fulfilled the required condition, the power of acceptance held by Gill would have been extinguished. When Claxton hit his shot, thereby "accepting" Barone's offer, Gill would have lost the opportunity to accept.

## Source

"Promising Prospects," *Sports Illustrated*, 3 July 2000, 41.

## References

*Plate v. Durst*, 24 S.E. 580 (1896).

RESTATEMENT (SECOND) OF CONTRACTS §§ 18, 29, 30, 223 (1981).

### § 18. Manifestation of Mutual Assent

Manifestation of mutual assent to an exchange requires that each party either make a promise or begin or render a performance.

### § 29. To Whom an Offer is Addressed

(1) The manifested intention of the offeror determines the person or persons in whom is created a power of acceptance.

(2) An offer may create a power of acceptance in a specified person or in one or more of a specified group or class of persons, acting separately or together, or in anyone or everyone who makes a specified promise or renders a specified performance.

## § 30. Form of Acceptance Invited

(1) An offer may invite or require acceptance to be made by an affirmative answer in words, or by performing or refraining from performing a specified act, or may empower the offeree to make a selection of terms in his acceptance.

(2) Unless otherwise indicated by the language or the circumstances, an offer invites acceptance in any manner and by any medium reasonable in the circumstances.

## § 223. Course of Dealing

(1) A course of dealing is a sequence of previous conduct between the parties to an agreement which is fairly to be regarded as establishing a common basis of understanding for interpreting their expressions and other conduct.

(2) Unless otherwise agreed, a course of dealing between the parties gives meaning to or supplements or qualifies their agreement.

# *Capacity to Contract*

## Dizzy and Paul

### Situation

In 1930, at the age of 19, future Hall of Fame pitcher Jay Hanna "Dizzy" Dean started one game for the St. Louis Cardinals, allowing one run in nine innings. Dean spent the next season in the minors, but the Cardinals promoted him to the big leagues for good in 1932. Once having made the Cardinals' roster for the 1932 season, Dean promptly proclaimed himself baseball's new "Wonder Boy." And although he had not yet spent a full season in the major leagues, the "Wonder Boy" was unhappy with his salary. In Dizzy's mind, his contract was not valid. Dean informed Sam Breadon, the Cardinals' owner, that he wanted to be released from his contract. To justify his demand, Dizzy invoked a fundamental principle of contract law. "I'm not yet twenty-one," he announced, "and my father didn't sign this year's contract like he did the others. So it's no good, and I'd like to be turned loose."

### Issue

If Dean had been under 21 at the time he signed his contract for the 1932 season, would he have been able to void the contract?

### Analysis

Dean had correctly construed the law of contracts. At the time, Missouri law considered any person under twenty-one to be a minor. In cases where a Missouri minor had signed a contract, the courts would have found the contract to be voidable. Dean, however, had difficulty separating fact from fiction. Though he was correct in his understanding of contract law, the facts were against him. The Cardinals' records showed Dean to be twenty-two years old. He was, therefore, legally capable of making fully binding contractual commitments. The team confronted him. "Yah," he said, coming clean, "I'm twenty-two all right. I musta been thinkin' of my brother Paul's birthday. He'll be twenty-two one of these days. Or is it twenty? Or nineteen? I reckon I'll have to ask him."

Dean would have had an even more difficult case under the law today. Consistent with § 14 of the Restatement of Contracts, Missouri now allows anyone eighteen years or older to enter into binding contracts. Under current law, all but three of the fifty states permit individuals who have reached the age of eighteen to enter into binding contracts. The exceptions are Mississippi, where the age of majority is twenty-one, and the states of Alabama and Nebraska, where the age of majority is nineteen.

---

## Source

Robert Gregory, *Diz: The Story of Dizzy Dean and Baseball during the Great Depression* (New York: Viking Penguin, 1992), 86.

## References

RESTATEMENT (SECOND) OF CONTRACTS §§ 12, 14 (1981).

### § 12. Capacity to Contract

(1) No one can be bound by contract who has no legal capacity to incur at least voidable contractual duties. Capacity to contract may be partial and its existence in respect of a particular transaction may depend upon the nature of the transaction or upon other circumstances.

(2) A natural person who manifests assent to a transaction has full legal capacity to incur contractual duties thereby unless he is

  (a)  under guardianship, or

  (b)  an infant, or

  (c)  mentally ill or defective, or

  (d)  intoxicated.

### § 14. Infants

Unless a statute provides otherwise, a natural person has the capacity to incur only voidable contractual duties until the beginning of the day before the person's eighteenth birthday.

# Crossing the Potomac

## Situation

In the early 1970s, 6'10" Moses Malone, a high school basketball star in Petersburg, Virginia, was pursued by more than 200 colleges and by pro scouts as well. The recruiting frenzy began when Malone scored 32 points in his first game with the Petersburg High School varsity. With each succeeding year in high school, Malone gained more attention, especially after he earned the highest possible rating at Garfinkel's Five-Star basketball summer camp following his junior year. In the spring of 1974, shortly before his high school graduation, Malone signed a letter of intent to attend the University of Maryland. At the same time that Maryland was pursuing Malone, Bucky Buckwalter, general manager of the Utah Stars of the American Basketball Association, was trying to persuade the phenom to skip college and head straight to the pros. In August 1974, Buckwalter and Jim Collier, the owner of the Stars, met with Malone at his house, spread ten $100 bills across an orange crate, and showed Malone a photograph of a Lincoln Mark IV. A short time later, while meeting with the Stars in the Washington, D.C. offices of his agent, Malone agreed to a five-year contract worth $590,000. There was one glitch: Malone was 19 years old at the time, and D.C. law required a person to be 21 in order to enter into a binding contract.

## Issue

Under the law of contracts, what options were available to Malone and the Utah Stars for purposes of entering into a fully binding contract?

## Analysis

At 19 years of age, Moses Malone lacked full legal capacity to enter into a binding contract in Washington, D.C. Consistent with §§ 12 and 14 of the Restatement of Contracts, Malone could enter into only a voidable contract in the District of Columbia. Signing Malone to a contract that he would later be able to void held little appeal for the Utah Stars. The only other available option was for Malone and the team's representatives to travel to a state that recognized the age of majority as 18 years of age. Conveniently, the state of Virginia permitted 18-year-olds to enter into valid contracts. After agreeing on compensation and other terms, Malone, his agent, and the officials from the Stars drove across the Potomac River to a Ramada Inn in Rosslyn, Virginia, where Malone signed the contract. With that, he became the first basketball player in history to go directly from high school to the pros.

## Source

Alexander Wolff, "The Road Not Taken," *Sports Illustrated*, 27 December 2004-3 January 2005.

## References

RESTATEMENT (SECOND) OF CONTRACTS §§ 12, 14 (1981).

### § 12. Capacity to Contract

(1) No one can be bound by contract who has no legal capacity to incur at least voidable contractual duties. Capacity to contract may be partial and its existence in respect of a particular transaction may depend upon the nature of the transaction or upon other circumstances.

(2) A natural person who manifests assent to a transaction has full legal capacity to incur contractual duties thereby unless he is

    (a)   under guardianship, or

    (b)  an infant, or

    (c)   mentally ill or defective, or

    (d)  intoxicated.

### § 14. Infants

Unless a statute provides otherwise, a natural person has the capacity to incur only voidable contractual duties until the beginning of the day before the person's eighteenth birthday.

# On the Town with Bad News Barnes

## Situation

After his junior year at Oregon State, basketball player Lonnie Shelton came to St. Louis to discuss signing a pro contract with the ABA's Spirits of St. Louis. While Shelton's agents were talking to the St. Louis management, Shelton went for a ride with 6'10" free spirit Marvin Barnes, then a center/forward with the St. Louis team. The two drove around St. Louis in Barnes' Rolls Royce. After being out with Barnes for a few hours, Shelton came back and signed a five-year contract at a salary of $150,000 per year. When Shelton returned to the Oregon State campus, he found that fans and school officials were outraged over his plans to leave school. Rumors circulated that Marvin Barnes had gotten Shelton drunk and that the inebriated Shelton had been coerced into signing the contract. Shelton began having severe misgivings about turning pro.

## Issues

If Shelton had been intoxicated when he signed the contract, would the Spirits have been able to enforce the agreement?

If Marvin Barnes had exercised undue influence over Shelton, would that fact have permitted Shelton to void the contract?

## Analysis

In many states, a person who is intoxicated by alcohol or use of drugs is considered incompetent to sign a contract. These states allow a person who does sign a contract while intoxicated to disavow the contract. Generally, the result is the same regardless of whether the person became drunk at a bar or took medication that impeded his thought processes. A smaller number of states allow a person who is intoxicated to get out of a contract only if the other party to the contract knows of the intoxication. If the Spirits had attempted to enforce the contract, Shelton's activities while in the company of Marvin Barnes would have played a significant role in determining whether the contract was valid.

Barnes was not a party to the contract. As to the issue of undue influence, therefore, it is doubtful that Shelton would have had a basis in law for voiding the contract even if Barnes had exercised undue influence. Under § 177(3) of the Restatement of Contracts, Shelton would not have been able to void the contract if the Spirits management, acting in good faith and without reason to know of the undue influence, either gave value to Shelton or relied materially on the transaction.

Rod Thorn, the coach of the Spirits at the time, was of the opinion that the contract was valid. "The kid wanted to sign," said Thorn, "he had excellent representation and he was going to get what, for that time, was huge money." Harry Weltman, the president of the Spirits, was of the same opinion. Weltman recalled that Shelton "went out with Marvin Barnes. Maybe they had a drink and maybe they didn't. They were only gone two or three hours and I don't know where they went or what they did." Marvin Barnes would admit only that he urged Shelton to sign the contract. Barnes had told Shelton, "Man, you're getting $150,000 a year, a house for your mother, a car. Boy, you better sign that damn contract. It's not as much as I'm making, but you're not as good as me."

Shelton signed and consternation broke out on the Oregon State campus. With the controversy building, the Spirits decided not to enforce the contract.

---

## Source

Terry Pluto, *Loose Balls: The Short, Wild Life of the American Basketball Association As Told by the Players, Coaches, and Movers and Shakers Who Made It Happen*, (New York: Simon & Schuster, 1990), 377.

## References

RESTATEMENT (SECOND) OF CONTRACTS §§ 16, 17, 177 (1981).

### § 16. Intoxicated Persons

A person incurs only voidable contractual duties by entering into a transaction if the other party has reason to know that by reason of intoxication (a) he is unable to understand in a reasonable manner the nature and consequences of the transaction, or (b) he is unable to act in a reasonable manner in relation to the transaction.

### § 17. Requirement of a Bargain

(1) Except as stated in Subsection (2), the formation of a contract requires a bargain in which there is a manifestation of mutual assent to the exchange and a consideration.

(2) Whether or not there is a bargain a contract may be formed under special rules applicable to formal contracts or under the rules stated in §§ 82-94.

### § 177. When Undue Influence Makes a Contract Voidable

(1) Undue influence is unfair persuasion of a party who is under the domination of the person exercising the persuasion or who by virtue of the relation between them is justified in assuming that that person will not act in a manner inconsistent with his welfare.

(2) If a party's manifestation of assent is induced by undue influence by the other party, the contract is voidable by the victim.

(3) If a party's manifestation of assent is induced by one who is not a party to the transaction, the contract is voidable by the victim unless the other party to the transaction in good faith and without reason to know of the undue influence either gives value or relies materially on the transaction.

# *Contract Formation*

## Jetting for Minnesota

### Situation

In March 2004, Antoine Winfield, a veteran of five years as a cornerback with the Buffalo Bills, appeared to have accepted a free-agent contract to play for the New York Jets. Winfield, together with his wife and two agents, visited the Jets' headquarters, met the team's owner and worked out a six-year, $30-million contract. Winfield toured the team's offices wearing a Jets jersey with "WINFIELD" and the number 26 on the back and made plans to attend the Jets' off-season workouts. However, when the Jets presented Winfield with the finished version of his written contract, he had second thoughts and declined to sign. A day later, Winfield flew to Minnesota and agreed to a six-year deal with the Vikings for $34.8 million.

### Issue

Under the law of contracts, did the New York Jets have a valid claim to Winfield's services?

### Analysis

Like most states, the state of New York has adopted a **Statute of Frauds**. Among other things, the Statute of Frauds provides that agreements extending for more than a year will not be enforced unless there is written evidence to support the agreement. The Statute of Frauds does not necessarily require a finished and signed contract. Under § 131 of the Restatement of Contracts, the requirement for a writing can be satisfied by a signed document indicating that a contract has been made and defining the terms of the contract with reasonable certainty. The required evidence can consist of a series of supporting documents, including unsigned papers that are clearly related to the transaction. A Jets jersey with "WINFIELD" on the back, however, falls short of the writing required. The contract discussions between Winfield and the Jets would fall under the category of preliminary negotiations, as that term is used in §§ 26 and 27 of the Restatement. Lacking a signed contract and apparently not having other supporting evidence, the Jets did not have a valid claim to Winfield's services.

## Source

Peter King, "March Madness," *Sports Illustrated*, 15 March 2004, 51–52.

## References

RESTATEMENT (SECOND) OF CONTRACTS §§ 26, 27, 38, 110, 131 (1981).

### § 26. Preliminary Negotiations

A manifestation of willingness to enter into a bargain is not an offer if the person to whom it is addressed knows or has reason to know that the person making it does not intend to conclude a bargain until he has made a further manifestation of assent.

### § 27. Existence of Contract Where Written Memorial Is Contemplated

Manifestations of assent that are in themselves sufficient to conclude a contract will not be prevented from so operating by the fact that the parties also manifest an intention to prepare and adopt a written memorial thereof; but the circumstances may show that the agreements are preliminary negotiations.

### § 38. Rejection

(1) An offeree's power of acceptance is terminated by his rejection of the offer, unless the offeror has manifested a contrary intention.

(2) A manifestation of intention not to accept an offer is a rejection unless the offeree manifests an intention to take it under further advisement.

### § 110. Classes of Contracts Covered [by the Statute of Frauds]

(1) The following classes of contracts are subject to a statute, commonly called the Statute of Frauds, forbidding enforcement unless there is a written memorandum or an applicable exception:

   (a) a contract of an executor or administrator to answer for a duty of his decedent (the executor-administrator provision);

   (b) a contract to answer for the duty of another (the suretyship provision);

   (c) a contract made upon consideration of marriage (the marriage provision);

   (d) a contract for the sale of an interest in land (the land contract provision);

   (e) a contract that is not to be performed within one year from the making thereof (the one-year provision).

## § 131. General Requisites of a Memorandum

Unless additional requirements are prescribed by the particular statute, a contract within the Statute of Frauds is enforceable if it is evidenced by any writing, signed by or on behalf of the party to be charged, which

(a) reasonably identifies the subject matter of the contract,

(b) is sufficient to indicate that a contact with respect thereto has been made between the parties or offered by the signer to the other party, and

(c) states with reasonable certainty the essential terms of the unperformed promises in the contract.

# Blaming Boozer

## Situation

By the summer of 2004, 6'8" forward Carlos Boozer was an NBA star in the making. The former Duke University standout had signed a two-year contract with the Cleveland Cavaliers before the 2002-03 season, his rookie year in the pros. The agreement gave the Cavaliers the option of extending Boozer's contract for a third year, 2004-05. If the Cavaliers exercised the option for 2004-05, they would have had to pay Boozer $695,000 for the year. If the Cavaliers declined to pick up the option, Boozer would become a restricted free agent. In that event, any NBA team would be free to offer Boozer a contract, although the Cavaliers would have the right to keep Boozer by matching the offer. The deadline for the Cavaliers to pick up the $695,000 option was midnight on June 30, 2004.

In a show of good faith in Boozer and with the intent of later signing him to a long-term contract, the Cavaliers elected not to pick up the option. For the Cavaliers, declining the option was a calculated risk; it meant that any other team was free to offer Boozer a contract. However, the Cavaliers believed they had an understanding with Boozer and his agent, Rob Pelinka, that Boozer would re-sign with Cleveland. The understanding was based on discussions that took place at a meeting in which Boozer reportedly told Cavaliers owner Gordon Gund and general manager Jim Paxson, "If you respect me by not picking up the option, I'll show trust and loyalty to you by signing with you."

Pursuant to the purported understanding, the Cavaliers allowed Boozer to become a free agent on July 1, 2004. Four days later, the Utah Jazz contacted Boozer's agent to inquire about the player's availability. Pelinka told the Jazz that Boozer had not committed to sign with Cleveland. Two days later, the Jazz worked out an agreement to pay Boozer $68 million over six years. When word got out that Boozer was negotiating with the Jazz, the Cavaliers and their fans were outraged. The team had clearly expected that Boozer would be a fixture in Cleveland for years to come. Facing financial constraints, the Cavaliers decided not to match Utah's offer and Boozer became a member of the Utah Jazz.

## Issue

Was there any legal basis upon which Cleveland could argue that Boozer was contractually obligated to sign with the Cavaliers?

## Analysis

The Cavaliers were simply out of luck. Depending on one's perspective, Carlos Boozer either outsmarted the Cavaliers management or failed to keep his word.

## 1. Option Contract

Clearly, the Cavaliers possessed a valid option for the 2004-05 season. Under § 87 of the Restatement of Contracts, an offer is binding as an option contract if it (1) is in writing and signed by the **offeror**, (2) recites a purported consideration for the making of the offer, and (3) proposes an exchange on fair terms within a reasonable time. Although the option was valid, the Cavaliers declined to exercise it.

## 2. "Unclean Hands"

The Collective Bargaining Agreement ("CBA") between NBA players and team owners prohibits teams from negotiating agreements with prospective free agents before the first day of July during a given year. The CBA also prohibits undisclosed agreements between teams and players. When the Cavaliers attempted to reach an "understanding" with Carlos Boozer in the days before the June 30th deadline, the team did so with full knowledge that the Collective Bargaining Agreement prohibited teams from signing restricted free agents to contracts until July 1. The Cavaliers were also aware that the NBA Constitution prohibited undisclosed agreements of any kind between teams and players, whether expressed, implied, oral, or written. The Cavaliers' conduct raises the issue of whether their dealings with Carlos Boozer amounted to misconduct under § 178 of the Restatement.

## 3. Statute of Frauds

By definition, a multi-year player contract is subject to the Statute of Frauds. Cases encompassed within the Statute of Frauds can be sued upon only if the agreement is evidenced by a writing that: (1) reasonably identifies the subject matter of the contract; (2) is sufficient to indicate that a contract has been made between the parties; and (3) states with reasonable certainty the essential terms of the unperformed promises in the contract. None of the parties to the "understanding" between Boozer and the Cavaliers suggested that there was a writing confirming Boozer's promise to show trust and loyalty to the Cavaliers. Even if the promise had been in writing, however, a commitment "to show trust and loyalty" is so vague as to be unenforceable.

## 4. Conclusion

The Cavaliers would not have been able to hold Carlos Boozer to the "understanding" because the agreement, if there was one, was: (1) tainted by the Cavaliers' misconduct; (2) not in writing; and (3) vague as to the essential terms.

---

## Sources

Brian Windhorst, "Boozer, Cavaliers Ready To Move On," *Akron Beacon Journal*, 14 July 2004.

Branson Wright, "Verbal Deal Could Mean Trouble," *The Cleveland Plain Dealer*, 14 July 2004.

## References

RESTATEMENT (SECOND) OF CONTRACTS §§ 25, 26, 87, 110, 178 (1981).

### § 25. Option Contracts

An option contract is a promise which meets the requirements for the formation of a contract and limits the promisor's power to revoke an offer.

### § 26. Preliminary Negotiations

A manifestation of willingness to enter into a bargain is not an offer if the person to whom it is addressed knows or has reason to know that the person making it does not intend to conclude a bargain until he has made a further manifestation of assent.

### § 87. Option Contract

(1)  An offer is binding as an option contract if it

   (a)  is in writing and signed by the offeror, recites a purported consideration for the making of the offer, and proposes an exchange on fair terms within a reasonable time; or

   (b)  is made irrevocable by statute.

(2)  An offer which the offeror should reasonably expect to induce action or forbearance of a substantial character on the part of the offeree before acceptance and which does induce such action or forbearance is binding as an option contract to the extent necessary to avoid injustice.

## § 110. Classes of Contracts Covered [by the Statute of Frauds]

(1) The following classes of contracts are subject to a statute, commonly called the Statute of Frauds, forbidding enforcement unless there is a written memorandum or an applicable exception:

(a) a contract of an executor or administrator to answer for a duty of his decedent (the executor-administrator provision);

(b) a contract to answer for the duty of another (the suretyship provision);

(c) a contract made upon consideration of marriage (the marriage provision);

(d) a contract for the sale of an interest in land (the land contract provision);

(e) a contract that is not to be performed within one year from the making thereof (the one-year provision).

## § 178. When a Term Is Unenforceable on Grounds of Public Policy

(1) A promise or other term of an agreement is unenforceable on grounds of public policy if legislation provides that it is unenforceable or the interest in its enforcement is clearly outweighed in the circumstances by a public policy against the enforcement of such terms.

(2) In weighing the interest in the enforcement of a term, account is taken of

(a) the parties' justified expectations,

(b) any forfeiture that would result if enforcement were denied, and

(c) any special public interest in the enforcement of the particular term.

(3) In weighing a public policy against enforcement of a term, account is taken of

(a) the strength of that policy as manifested by legislation or judicial decisions,

(b) the likelihood that a refusal to enforce the term will further that policy,

(c) the seriousness of any misconduct involved and the extent to which it was deliberate, and

(d) the directness of the connection between that misconduct and the term.

# Booked for Seattle

## Situation

Seattle's Safeco Field was the site of the 2001 major league baseball all-star game. In the days before the game, Florida Marlins outfielder Cliff Floyd spent nearly $16,000 to buy airplane tickets to Seattle so that his family and friends could watch him play. Floyd was certain he would be selected to play for the National League team. Not only did he have a .341 batting average, sixth best in the league, and 70 runs batted in, he also had what he thought was a commitment from the National League manager, Bobby Valentine. Floyd had spoken with Valentine on the telephone before the manager announced his selection of the reserves for the NL team. Floyd received the distinct impression from the conversation that Valentine intended to pick Floyd as a reserve. Floyd thought Valentine's assurance was ironclad. Valentine disagreed. Floyd "misunderstood the conversation," Valentine said. Floyd was adamant, however. "If he said I misunderstood, then he's lying," the player declared. According to Floyd, Valentine had told him that he was on the team "if nothing crazy happens in the next 24 hours."

## Issue

Did Cliff Floyd have a legal right to insist that Valentine select him for the All-Star team?

## Analysis

Whatever Valentine said in the phone conversation with Floyd, it was, at most, a moral commitment and far short of an enforceable contract. However, by analogy, the case provides insight into the doctrine of "promissory estoppel."

If Bobby Valentine had extended a bona fide offer to Cliff Floyd, and if Floyd—in reasonable reliance on the offer—had spent $16,000 preparing to respond before Valentine revoked the offer, the law might well have implied a contract. Professor Samuel Williston, a prominent legal scholar during the 1920s, wrote "it may fairly be argued that the fundamental basis of simple contracts historically was action in justifiable reliance on a promise." The Restatement of Contracts, § 87(2), provides that if an offeror makes an offer that is reasonably expected to induce substantial action or forbearance, and if the **offeree** does act or forbear from acting, then the offer becomes a binding option contract to the extent necessary to prevent injustice. The most important question to be answered was whether Floyd's reliance on Valentine's assurance was justifiable. If so, a court might have been inclined to hold Valentine to his promise, *i.e.*, to "estop" him from reneging on that promise.

Ultimately, Valentine did find a way to accommodate Floyd. Mets pitcher Rick Reed, whom Valentine had selected for the team, came up with a stiff neck in the days before the all-star game. Valentine named Floyd to take Reed's spot.

## Sources

"All-Star Spat," *The Washington Post*, 6 July 2001, D7.

"Floyd Named to NL Squad: Valentine's Late Pick Extends Mini-Drama," *The Washington Post*, 9 July 2001, D7.

## References

RESTATEMENT (SECOND) OF CONTRACTS §§ 34, 87, 344 (1981).

### § 34. Certainty and Choice of Terms; Effect of Performance or Reliance

(1) The terms of a contract may be reasonably certain even though it empowers one or both parties to make a selection of terms in the course of performance.

(2) Part performance under an agreement may remove uncertainty and establish that a contract enforceable as a bargain has been formed.

(3) Action in reliance on an agreement may make a contractual remedy appropriate even though uncertainty is not removed.

### § 87. Option Contract

(1) An offer is binding as an option contract if it

    (a) is in writing and signed by the offeror, recites a purported consideration for the making of the offer, and proposes an exchange on fair terms within a reasonable time; or

    (b) is made irrevocable by statute.

(2) An offer which the offeror should reasonably expect to induce action or forbearance of a substantial character on the part of the offeree before acceptance and which does induce such action or forbearance is binding as an option contract to the extent necessary to avoid injustice.

### § 344. Purposes of Remedies

Judicial remedies under the rules stated in this Restatement serve to protect one or more of the following interests of a promisee:

(a) his "expectation interest," which is his interest in having the benefit of his bargain by being put in as good a position as he would have been in had the contract been performed,

(b) his "reliance interest," which is his interest in being reimbursed for loss caused by reliance on the contract by being put in as good a position as he would have been in had the contract not been made, or

(c) his "restitution interest," which is his interest in having restored to him any benefit that he has conferred on the other party.

# Short-Term Employment

## Situation

On Monday, November 1, 2004, former New York Mets second baseman Wally Backman reached an oral agreement with the Arizona Diamondbacks baseball team to serve as the team's manager for the 2005 and 2006 seasons. Four days later, Backman was out of a job, the victim of a few skeletons in his closet. Unbeknownst to the Diamondbacks, Backman's police record included a conviction for driving under the influence of alcohol and a guilty plea to charges stemming from a fight. During Backman's final interview for the job, Diamondbacks' officials asked him if he had any record of past conduct that would cause problems. He assured them that he did not. The Diamondbacks learned of Backman's legal troubles only after newspapers checked his court records. Backman was not in the employ of the Diamondbacks long enough even to sign a written contract.

## Issue

What legal justification could the Arizona Diamondbacks have asserted as the basis for the decision to fire Backman?

## Analysis

There was an oral employment agreement between Backman and the Diamondbacks. However, under terms of the agreement, Backman was to manage the team for two years, so the Arizona Statute of Frauds would have required the contract to be in writing. From a legal perspective, Backman and the Diamondbacks never had a legally binding employment agreement. Therefore, in accordance with § 110 of the Restatement of Contracts, the employment agreement that Backman negotiated with the Diamondbacks would not have been enforceable. The team did not have to fire him because he was never formally hired. Even if there had been a written employment agreement, § 164 of the Restatement would have provided a basis on which the team could have voided the contract. But for misrepresentation, the Diamondbacks would not have decided to hire Backman.

## Source

Jack Curry, "The Past Costs Backman His Job, Four Days After He Received It," *The N.Y. Times*, 6 November 2004, D1.

## References

RESTATEMENT (SECOND) OF CONTRACTS §§ 42, 110, 159, 161, 162, 163, 164 (1981).

### § 42. Revocation by Communication From Offeror Received by Offeree

An offeree's power of acceptance is terminated when the offeree receives from the offeror a manifestation of an intention not to enter into the proposed contract.

### § 110. Classes of Contracts Covered [by the Statute of Frauds]

(1) The following classes of contracts are subject to a statute, commonly called the Statute of Frauds, forbidding enforcement unless there is a written memorandum or an applicable exception:

    (a) a contract of an executor or administrator to answer for a duty of his decedent (the executor-administrator provision);

    (b) a contract to answer for the duty of another (the suretyship provision);

    (c) a contract made upon consideration of marriage (the marriage provision);

    (d) a contract for the sale of an interest in land (the land contract provision);

    (e) a contract that is not to be performed within one year from the making thereof (the one-year provision).

### § 159. Misrepresentation Defined

A misrepresentation is an assertion that is not in accord with the facts.

### § 161. When Non-disclosure Is Equivalent to an Assertion

A person's non-disclosure of a fact known to him is equivalent to an assertion that the fact does not exist in the following cases only:

    (a) where he knows that disclosure of the fact is necessary to prevent some previous assertion from being a misrepresentation or from being fraudulent or material.

    (b) where he knows that disclosure of the fact would correct a mistake of the other party as to a basic assumption on which that party is making the contract and if non-disclosure of the fact amounts to a failure to act in good faith and in accordance with reasonable standards of fair dealing.

(c) where he knows that disclosure of the fact would correct a mistake of the other party as to the contents or effect of a writing, evidencing or embodying an agreement in whole or in part.

(d) where the other person is entitled to know the fact because of a relation of trust and confidence between them.

## § 162. When a Misrepresentation Is Fraudulent or Material

(1) A misrepresentation is fraudulent if the maker intends his assertion to induce a party to manifest his assent and the maker:

(a) knows or believes that the assertion is not in accord with the facts, or

(b) does not have the confidence that he states or implies in the truth of the assertion, or

(c) knows that he does not have the basis that he states or implies for the assertion.

(2) A misrepresentation is material if it would be likely to induce a reasonable person to manifest his assent, or if the maker knows that it would be likely to induce the recipient to do so.

## § 163. When a Misrepresentation Prevents Formation of a Contract

If a misrepresentation as to the character or essential terms of a proposed contract induces conduct that appears to be a manifestation of assent by one who neither knows nor has reasonable opportunity to know of the character or essential terms of the proposed contract, his conduct is not effective as a manifestation of assent.

## § 164. When a Misrepresentation Makes a Contract Voidable

(1) If a party's manifestation of assent is induced by either a fraudulent or a material misrepresentation by the other party upon which the recipient is justified in relying, the contract is voidable by the recipient.

(2) If a party's manifestation of assent is induced by either a fraudulent or a material misrepresentation by one who is not a party to the transaction upon which the recipient is justified in relying, the contract is voidable by the recipient, unless the other party to the transaction in good faith and without reason to know of the misrepresentation either gives value or relies materially on the transaction.

# Taking Care of Hurricane Hazle

## Situation

Bob "Hurricane" Hazle, a former outfielder for the Milwaukee Braves, was a one-season sensation. 1957 was his year. Thousands of major league ballplayers have enjoyed longer careers than Bob Hazle. Relatively few, however, have garnered as many headlines as Hazle did. For a brief period in the summer and fall of 1957, Hazle attained near-mythical status. Thrust into the Braves' starting lineup by an injury to center fielder Billy Bruton, Hazle played in 41 games and went to bat 134 times. The results were extraordinary. Hazle hit seven home runs, with a .403 batting average and 27 runs batted in. No one, not Hazle and certainly not the Braves organization, expected such feats. Playing at the minimum major league salary of $6,000, Hazle was a real bargain. Once it became obvious that Hazle had earned a spot in the Braves' lineup, he asked general manager John Quinn for a raise in pay. "He kept telling me he'd take care of me," Hazle said long after his career had ended. "You're going great, you're going great," the general manager told Hazle, "and I'm going to take care of you." At season's end, after the Braves had defeated the New York Yankees to win the World Series, Quinn handed Hazle a "bonus" check for an additional $1,000. The check was far from adequate compensation for Hazle's contributions. Hazle promptly gave the check back to Quinn and drove home to South Carolina.

## Issue

Under the law of contracts, did John Quinn's promise to "take care of" Bob Hazle constitute an enforceable agreement?

## Analysis

Without mutual obligations and legal consideration, Quinn's assurance that he would take care of Hazle was merely a **naked promise**. Sadly for Hazle, there was no enforceable agreement. As he recognized, he had no choice but to pick up his bags and go home. Under § 89 of the Restatement of Contracts, a promise that modifies a duty under a contract that has not been fully performed will, under certain circumstances, be binding on both sides. However, the modification must be fair and equitable and prompted by circumstances that were not anticipated when the original contract was made. The unanticipated circumstances that would support a modification typically consist of additional efforts required of the promisee. Although the Braves did not anticipate Hazle's spectacular play, his

.403 average did not constitute the sort of unanticipated circumstances that would support a modification of his contract.

Under § 71 of the Restatement of Contracts, a relationship between two persons does not ripen into a contractual relationship if there exists only a naked promise that was induced by the conduct of the promisee. For a valid modification of contract, the relationship must be two-way, *i.e.*, Hazle's future performance would have to be sought by Quinn in exchange for his promise of a bonus and Hazle would have to give that performance in exchange for Quinn's promise. In fact, Quinn's promise did not induce Hazle to undertake any new or additional performance; he was already contractually obligated to play for the Braves.

The Braves may have had a moral obligation to pay Hazle more money. However, § 86 of the Restatement of Contracts makes it clear that moral obligations based solely on gratitude or sentiment are not sufficient to support a subsequent promise. Under § 86, a promise made in recognition of a benefit previously received by the promisor from the promisee is binding to the extent necessary to prevent injustice. Though Bob Hazle may have thought it was an injustice to be playing for the Braves for a mere $6,000, the law would ask whether the Braves had been unjustly enriched. The clear answer is that there was no unjust enrichment. The Braves had contracted to pay Hazle $6,000 for his performance, whether he performed well or badly. Under § 73 of the Restatement, the performance of a legal duty owed to a promisor which is neither doubtful nor the subject of honest dispute cannot form valid consideration for new terms or a new agreement.

The result might well have been different if John Quinn had put his promise in writing. Under § 95, if there were no statute that otherwise governed, Quinn's promise would have been binding, even without an additional performance from Hurricane Hazle, if (1) the promise was in writing and sealed; (2) the writing was delivered to Hazle; and (3) the Braves and Hazle were both named in the writing.

## Source

Skip Rosin, *One Step From Glory: On the Fringe of Professional Sports* (New York: Simon and Schuster, 1979), 210–11.

## References

RESTATEMENT (SECOND) OF CONTRACTS §§ 33, 71, 73, 86, 89, 95 (1981).

## § 33. Certainty

(1) Even though a manifestation of intention is intended to be understood as an offer, it cannot be accepted so as to form a contract unless the terms of the contract are reasonably certain.

(2) The terms of a contract are reasonably certain if they provide a basis for determining the existence of a breach and for giving an appropriate remedy.

(3) The fact that one or more terms of a proposed bargain are left open or uncertain may show that a manifestation of intention is not intended to be understood as an offer or as an acceptance.

## § 71. Requirement of Exchange; Types of Exchange

(1) To constitute consideration, a performance or a return promise must be bargained for.

(2) A performance or return promise is bargained for if it is sought by the promisor in exchange for his promise and is given by the promisee in exchange for that promise.

(3) The performance may consist of

    (a) an act other than a promise, or

    (b) a forbearance, or

    (c) the creation, modification, or destruction of a legal relation.

(4) The performance or return promise may be given to the promisor or to some other person. It may be given by the promisee or by some other person.

## § 73. Performance of a Legal Duty

Performance of a legal duty owed to a promisor which is neither doubtful nor the subject of honest dispute is not consideration; but a similar performance is consideration if it differs from what was required by the duty in a way which reflects more than a pretense of bargain.

## § 86. Promise for Benefit Received

(1) A promise made in recognition of a benefit previously received by the promisor from the promisee is binding to the extent necessary to prevent injustice.

(2) A promise is not binding under Subsection (1)

    (a) if the promisee conferred the benefit as a gift or for other reasons the promisor has not been unjustly enriched; or

    (b) to the extent that its value is disproportionate to the benefit.

## § 89. Modification of Executory Contract

A promise modifying a duty under a contract not fully performed on either side is binding:

(a) if the modification is fair and equitable in view of circumstances not anticipated by the parties when the contract was made; or

(b) to the extent provided by statute; or

(c) to the extent that justice requires enforcement in view of material change of position in reliance on the promise.

## § 95. Requirements for Sealed Contract or Written Contract or Instrument

(1) In the absence of statute a promise is binding without consideration if

(a) it is in writing and sealed; and

(b) the document containing the promise is delivered; and

(c) the promisor and promisee are named in the document or so described as to be capable of identification when it is delivered.

(2) When a statute provides in effect that a written contract or instrument is binding without consideration or that lack of consideration is an affirmative defense to an action on a written contract or instrument, in order to be subject to the statute a promise must either

(a) be expressed in a document signed or otherwise assented to by the promisor and delivered; or

(b) be expressed in a writing or writings to which both promisor and promisee manifest assent.

# Men's Room Contract

## Situation

Tom Heinsohn, a 6'7" forward for the Boston Celtics in the 1950s and 1960s, once negotiated a contract with the Celtics' owner, Walter Brown, while the two stood side-by-side in the men's room of a Boston restaurant. "He asked what I wanted, and I told him," Heinsohn said. "We made the deal before we zipped up."

## Issue

Is a conversation in the men's room of a Boston restaurant sufficient to form a valid contract?

## Analysis

Section 27 of the Restatement of Contracts recognizes that two or more parties may enter into a binding agreement even before the terms of the deal are memorialized in a written document. On the other hand, it is also possible that an oral exchange between two or more parties is merely a preliminary negotiation, in which case the parties would not be bound until there is a written final expression of the agreement. If either party knows that the other party regards the contract talks as incomplete or that the other party does not want to be bound until the contract is in written form, the discussions would not constitute a binding contract.

When Tom Heinsohn and Walter Brown held contract discussions side-by-side in the men's room, it was clear to both parties that they were concluding a final agreement. The oral contract would certainly have included an agreement by both men that they would later sign a formal writing. However, under § 27, Heinsohn's commitment to play one more year for the Celtics, and Brown's commitment to employ Heinsohn for that year, became an enforceable agreement even before the two walked out of the men's room. A simple "yes" uttered in the men's room of a Boston restaurant suffices to create an oral or **parol contract**.

The provision of the Statute of Frauds requiring written evidence of contracts that cannot be performed within one year would not have come into play. In the era in which Heinsohn played, player contracts were typically negotiated and signed on a year-by-year basis.

## Source

Mark Bechtel, "Catching Up With Tom Heinsohn, Celtics Forward," *Sports Illustrated*, 8 February 1999, 12.

## Reference

RESTATEMENT (SECOND) OF CONTRACTS § 27 (1981).

### § 27. Existence of Contract Where Written Memorial is Contemplated

Manifestations of assent that are in themselves sufficient to conclude a contract will not be prevented from so operating by the fact that the parties also manifest an intention to prepare and adopt a written memorial thereof; but the circumstances may show that the agreements are preliminary negotiations.

# If Not for Paragraph Six...

## Situation

When the American Basketball Association was formed in 1966, one of its strategies was to attempt to sign players from the rival National Basketball Association. The ABA franchise in the Bay Area, the Oakland Oaks, pursued Rick Barry, then a star with the NBA's San Francisco Warriors. The Oaks offered Barry $75,000 a year in salary and 15% ownership of the team. During the negotiations, Barry made it clear to team owners Pat Boone and Ken Davidson that he enjoyed living in the San Francisco Bay Area and wanted to remain there. The owners assured Barry that if the team ever moved away from Oakland, he would not be obligated to continue playing for the team. The assurance was not reflected in Barry's written contract with the Oaks, however. To the contrary, paragraph 6 of the agreement stated, "the Club shall have the right to sell, exchange, assign and transfer this contract to any other professional basketball club in the Association and the Player agrees to accept such assignment and to faithfully perform and carry out this contract with the same force and effect as if it had been entered into by the Player with the assignee Club instead of with this Club."

By the end of the team's second year in Oakland, the franchise was facing financial disaster. Boone and Davidson sold the team to avert bankruptcy. The new owner, Earl Foreman, moved the team to Washington, D.C. and changed its name to the Washington Capitols. Relying upon the verbal agreement, Barry thought he was relieved of his contractual obligation to the team. So, with two years remaining on his contract with the Oaks, he worked out a five-year contract to play for his old team, the Warriors.

## Issue

Under paragraph 6 of his contract with the Oakland Oaks, was Rick Barry obligated to play for the Washington Capitols?

## Analysis

Sections 359 and 367 of the Restatement of Contracts reflect a pronounced distaste for awarding specific performance as a remedy for breach of contract. Section 359(1) provides that specific performance will not be ordered if monetary damages would be adequate to protect the injured party. Courts are reluctant to compel athletes to perform, against their will, for professional teams. As a general rule, the judicial system finds it undesirable to require an athlete to wear the uniform of an employer after the bond of loyalty has been impaired. For this reason, in breach of contract cases, courts will typically consider other feasible remedies in lieu of awarding specific performance.

The converse of the principle set forth in § 359(1) is that courts may require specific performance when monetary damages would not provide adequate compensation. In *Washington Capitols Basketball Club, Inc. v. Barry*, the court looked at the feasibility of monetary damages. The court concluded, however, that the Washington Capitols would suffer irreparable injury if deprived of Rick Barry's talents. In the court's view, irreparable injury results when no amount of money can compensate a team for the loss of an "irreplaceable athlete." The court found Barry to be an irreplaceable athlete.

The court held, therefore, that Barry could not play for the Warriors until he had fulfilled the contract he signed with the Oaks. And, notwithstanding Barry's verbal agreement with the Oaks' owners, the court found that the terms of his written contract required him to play for any team to which the Oaks assigned the contract. Having lost the court case, Barry got into his car, drove across the country, and played for the Washington Capitols.

## Source

*Washington Capitols Basketball Club, Inc. v. Barry*, 304 F.Supp. 1193 (N.D. Cal. 1969).

## References

RESTATEMENT (SECOND) OF CONTRACTS §§ 317, 345, 359, 360, 367 (1981).

### § 317. Assignment of a Right

(1) An assignment of a right is a manifestation of the assignor's intention to transfer it by virtue of which the assignor's right to performance by the obligor is extinguished in whole or in part and the assignee acquires a right to such performance.

(2) A contractual right can be assigned unless:

    (a) the substitution of a right of the assignee for the right of the assignor would materially change the duty of the obligor, or materially increase the burden or risk imposed on him by his contract, or materially impair his chance of obtaining return performance, or materially reduce its value to him, or

    (b) the assignment is forbidden by statute or is otherwise inoperative on grounds of public policy, or

    (c)   assignment is validly precluded by contract.

## § 345. Judicial Remedies Available

The judicial remedies available for the protection of the interests stated in § 344 include a judgment or order

    (a)   awarding a sum of money due under the contract or as damages,

    (b)   requiring specific performance of a contract or enjoining its non-performance,

    (c)   requiring restoration of a specific thing to prevent unjust enrichment,

    (d)   awarding a sum of money to prevent unjust enrichment,

    (e)   declaring the rights of the parties, and

    (f)   enforcing an arbitration award.

## § 359. Effect of Adequacy of Damages

(1)   Specific performance or an injunction will not be ordered if damages would be adequate to protect the expectation interest of the injured party.

(2)   The adequacy of the damage remedy for failure to render one part of the performance due does not preclude specific performance or injunction as to the contract as a whole.

(3)   Specific performance or an injunction will not be refused merely because there is a remedy for breach other than damages, but such a remedy may be considered in exercising discretion under the rule stated in § 357.

## § 360. Factors Affecting Adequacy of Damages

In determining whether the remedy in damages would be adequate, the following circumstances are significant:

    (a)   the difficulty of proving damages with reasonable certainty,

    (b)   the difficulty of procuring a suitable substitute performance by means of money awarded as damages, and

    (c)   the likelihood that an award of damages could not be collected.

## § 367. Contracts for Personal Service or Supervision

(1)   A promise to render personal service will not be specifically enforced.

(2)   A promise to render personal service exclusively for one employer will not be enforced by an injunction against serving another if its probable result will be to compel a performance involving personal relations the enforced continuance of

which is undesirable or will be to leave the employee without other reasonable means of making a living.

# The Anti-Cracker Clause

## Situation

Hall-of-Fame pitcher Rube Waddell played for Connie Mack's Philadelphia Athletics from 1902 to 1907. Waddell was fond of eating crackers in bed, a habit which gave rise to a labor relations issue for Mack. In Waddell's era, baseball players slept two to a bed when staying in hotels on road trips. Waddell's bedmate complained bitterly about the cracker crumbs that Waddell would leave in the bed. In lieu of giving the pitcher a bed all to himself, Mack inserted a clause into Waddell's contract prohibiting him from eating crackers in bed.

## Issue

Under the law of contracts, was the "anti-cracker" clause in Waddell's contract a valid and enforceable provision?

## Analysis

Under § 71(3), a forbearance, even a forbearance from eating crackers, is a valid subject for a contract. In signing his contract, Waddell voluntarily gave up something that was of value to him. The "anti-cracker" clause satisfied the threshold requirement for consideration; it was a performance that was sought by Connie Mack in an exchange that was bargained for. The provision was valid and enforceable.

## Source

George F. Will, *Bunts: Curt Flood, Camden Yards, Pete Rose and Other Reflections on Baseball* (New York: Scribner, 1998), 129.

## Reference

RESTATEMENT (SECOND) OF CONTRACTS § 71 (1981).

### § 71. Requirement of Exchange; Types of Exchange

(1)  To constitute consideration, a performance or a return promise must be bargained for.

(2)  A performance or return promise is bargained for if it is sought by the promisor in exchange for his promise and is given by the promisee in exchange for that promise.

(3) The performance may consist of

    (a) an act other than a promise, or

    (b) a forbearance, or

    (c) the creation, modification, or destruction of a legal relation.

(4) The performance or return promise may be given to the promisor or to some other person. It may be given by the promisee or by some other person.

# A Passing Inducement

## Situation

When Clemson University football coach Tommy Bowden was recruiting Roscoe Crosby, a wide receiver of great promise, Bowden resorted to a unique inducement. He promised Crosby that if he enrolled at Clemson, the team's first offensive play of the 2001 season would be a pass to Crosby.

## Issue

If Crosby did enroll at Clemson and Bowden had called a running play on the first play of the 2001 season, what remedy, if any, would be available to Crosby?

## Analysis

Crosby did accept Bowden's offer. Under § 71 of the Restatement of Contracts, the commitment would be viewed as enforceable. The promise of a pass play was something for which Crosby had bargained.

For Bowden, it was not a commitment made lightly. "You've got to be careful what you promise," the Clemson coach commented, because "you can't make the same promise to everybody." Bowden made good on his promise. Clemson's first play in the opening game of its 2001 season was a pass to Crosby, good for a 12-yard gain.

Under § 241 of the Restatement, if Bowden had called a running play to start the 2001 season, the breach would likely not have been considered a material breach. If Crosby had filed a claim for breach of contract, a court would likely have determined that there was no significant harm to Crosby as long as Clemson fulfilled its promise to him of a four-year scholarship.

## Source

Josh Barr, "Promises to Keep," *The Washington Post*, 3 September 2001, D3.

## References

RESTATEMENT (SECOND) OF CONTRACTS §§ 24, 71, 205, 235, 241 (1981).

## § 24. Offer Defined

An offer is the manifestation of willingness to enter into a bargain, so made as to justify another person in understanding that his assent to that bargain is invited and will conclude it.

## § 71. Requirement of Exchange; Types of Exchange

(1) To constitute consideration, a performance or a return promise must be bargained for.

(2) A performance or return promise is bargained for if it is sought by the promisor in exchange for his promise and is given by the promisee in exchange for that promise.

(3) The performance may consist of

(a) an act other than a promise, or

(b) a forbearance, or

(c) the creation, modification, or destruction of a legal relation.

(4) The performance or return promise may be given to the promisor or to some other person. It may be given by the promisee or by some other person.

## § 205. Duty of Good Faith and Fair Dealing

Every contract imposes upon each party a duty of good faith and fair dealing in its performance and its enforcement.

## § 235. Effect of Performance as Discharge and of Non-Performance as Breach

(1) Full performance of a duty under a contract discharges the duty.

(2) When performance of a duty under a contract is due any non-performance is a breach.

## § 241. Circumstances Significant in Determining Whether a Failure Is Material

In determining whether a failure to render or to offer performance is material, the following circumstances are significant:

(a) the extent to which the injured party will be deprived of the benefit which he reasonably expected;

(b) the extent to which the injured party can be adequately compensated for the part of that benefit of which he will be deprived;

(c) the extent to which the party failing to perform or to offer to perform will suffer forfeiture;

(d) the likelihood that the party failing to perform or to offer to perform will cure his failure, taking into account of all the circumstances including any reasonable assurances;

(e) the extent to which the behavior of the party failing to perform or to offer to perform comports with standards of good faith and fair dealing.

# Grieving Over $6.5 Million

## Situation

On December 26, 2003, the agent for Pro Bowl linebacker LaVar Arrington signed a contract extension with the Washington Redskins on Arrington's behalf. The contract extension would pay Arrington $68 million over eight years. A month after the contract was signed, Arrington and his agent, Carl Poston, claimed that a provision calling for a $6.5 million roster bonus in 2006 was inadvertently left out of the final agreement. In explaining the "missing" bonus, Arrington accused the Redskins of removing the roster bonus language from the final text of the agreement. Arrington explained that, due to deadline pressure, Poston didn't have a chance to properly review the entire contract. The Redskins denied any wrongdoing. A Redskins spokesman remarked, "What's the deception in a drafted and signed contract?" The Redskins said that language relating to the roster bonus did not appear in earlier versions of the contract that Poston had initialed. Arrington filed a formal grievance against the Redskins, seeking a determination that the team was obligated to pay the $6.5 million bonus.

## Issue

Are the Redskins likely to be successful in their bid to uphold the terms reflected in the signed agreement and exclude the $6.5 million bonus?

## Analysis

The contract extension signed by Arrington's agent and the Redskins covered a period of eight years. Accordingly, under §§ 110 and 130 of the Restatement of Contracts, all promises to be included in the contract would have to be put into writing. The Redskins assert that the signed contract is an **integrated agreement** under § 209 of the Restatement and therefore a "final expression" of the deal. Arrington would have the burden of demonstrating that the document his agent signed was not, in fact, an integrated agreement. To do so, he would have to prove that the Redskins engaged in fraud. Under § 214 of the Restatement, this showing would require evidence, through prior or contemporaneous agreements or negotiations, that the Redskins had agreed to the roster bonus and then purposely removed the bonus language from the contract without the linebacker's consent. In the event Arrington could show that the Redskins had removed the bonus language without consent, he would prevail. Absent fraud or bad faith by the Redskins, however, it is likely that the contract would be upheld as an integrated agreement under § 209.

## Sources

Nunyo Demasio, "Redskins' Arrington Has Filed Grievance," *The Washington Post*, 15 March 2004, D3.

Nunyo Demasio, "Arrington, Redskins Going to Arbitration; $6.5M Bonus Is Being Disputed," *The Washington Post*, 9 July 2004, D1.

## References

RESTATEMENT (SECOND) OF CONTRACTS §§ 110, 130, 134, 205, 209, 214 (1981).

### § 110. Classes of Contracts Covered

(1) The following classes of contracts are subject to a statute, commonly called the Statute of Frauds, forbidding enforcement unless there is a written memorandum or an applicable exception:

    (a) a contract of an executor or administrator to answer for a duty of his decedent (the executor-administrator provision);

    (b) a contract to answer for the duty of another (the suretyship provision);

    (c) a contract made upon consideration of marriage (the marriage provision);

    (d) a contract for the sale of an interest in land (the land contract provision);

    (e) a contract that is not to be performed within one year from the making thereof (the one-year provision).

(2) The following classes of contracts, which were traditionally subject to the Statute of Frauds, are now governed by Statute of Frauds provisions of the Uniform Commercial Code:

    (a) a contract for the sale of goods for the price of $500 or more (Uniform Commercial Code § 2-201);

    (b) a contract for the sale of securities (Uniform Commercial Code § 8-319);

    (c) a contract for the sale of personal property not otherwise covered, to the extent of enforcement by way or action or defense beyond $5,000 in amount or value of remedy (Uniform Commercial Code § 1-206).

(3) In addition the Uniform Commercial Code requires a writing signed by the debtor for an agreement which creates or provides for a security interest in personal property or fixtures not in the possession of the secured party.

(4) Statutes in most states provide that no acknowledgment or promise is sufficient evidence of a new or continuing contract to take a case out of the operation of a statute of limitations unless made in some writing signed by the party to be charged, but that the statute does not alter the effect of any payment of principal or interest.

(5) In many states other classes of contracts are subject to a requirement of a writing.

## § 130. Contract Not to Be Performed Within a Year

(1) Where any promise in a contract cannot be fully performed within a year from the time the contract is made, all promises in the contract are within the Statute of Frauds until one party to the contract completes his performance.

(2) When one party to a contract has completed his performance, the one-year provision of the Statute does not prevent enforcement of the promises of other parties.

## § 134. Signature [Under the Statute of Frauds]

The signature to a memorandum may be any symbol made or adopted with an intention, actual or apparent, to authenticate the writing as that of the signer.

## § 205. Duty of Good Faith and Fair Dealing

Every contract imposes upon each party a duty of good faith and fair dealing in its performance and its enforcement.

## § 209. Integrated Agreements

(1) An integrated agreement is a writing or writings constituting a final expression of one or more terms of an agreement.

(2) Whether there is an integrated agreement is to be determined by the court as a question preliminary to determination of a question of interpretation or to application of the parol evidence rule.

(3) Where the parties reduce an agreement to a writing which in view of its completeness and specificity reasonably appears to be a complete agreement, it is taken to be an integrated agreement unless it is established by other evidence that the writing did not constitute a final expression.

## § 214. Evidence of Prior or Contemporaneous Agreements and Negotiations

Agreements and negotiations prior to or contemporaneous with the adoption of a writing are admissible in evidence to establish

(a) that the writing is or is not an integrated agreement;

(b) that the integrated agreement, if any, is completely or partially integrated;

(c) the meaning of the writing, whether or not integrated;

(d) illegality, fraud, duress, mistake, lack of consideration, or other invalidating cause;

(e) ground for granting or denying rescission, reformation, specific performance, or other remedy.

# Just the Fax

## Situation

The New Jersey Devils of the National Hockey League thought they had winger Claude Lemieux, the Most Valuable Player of the 1994-1995 NHL playoffs, signed and sealed for the 1995-1996 season. On June 30, 1995, Lemieux signed a copy of a contract that the Devils had sent to him over the fax machine. Under the contract, the Devils were to pay Lemieux $5.2 million for four years. Weeks later, Lemieux had second thoughts. He informed the Devils that his contract wasn't valid because he had signed a fax copy, not the original document. When Lemieux failed to report for the start of the new season, the Devils took the case to a hearing before an arbitrator in an effort to enforce the contract.

## Issue

Under the law of contracts, did the fax copy that Claude Lemieux signed constitute a valid contract?

## Analysis

Not surprisingly, the arbitrator ruled in favor of the Devils. The only real surprise was that the hearing lasted two days and consumed seventeen hours. The arbitrator's ruling established that a facsimile copy of a contract is as good as the original. In signing the fax, it was as if Lemieux had signed the original document. "We're not at all surprised by today's ruling," Lou Lamoriello, president and general manager of the club, said in a statement after the arbitrator's decision. "We've been saying all along that as far as we are concerned, Claude Lemieux was under contract to the New Jersey Devils." Under § 209 of the Restatement of Contracts, if two or more parties put an agreement in writing which appears to be a complete agreement, it is taken to be an integrated agreement unless other evidence shows that the writing was not a final expression of the contract.

## Source

Alex Yannis, "Devils Win Lemieux Case," *The N.Y. Times*, 30 September 1995, Sec. 1, 29.

## References

RESTATEMENT (SECOND) OF CONTRACTS §§ 1, 71, 209 (1981).

### § 1. Contract Defined

A contract is a promise or a set of promises for the breach of which the law gives a remedy, or the performance of which the law in some way recognizes as a duty.

### § 71. Requirement of Exchange; Types of Exchange

(1) To constitute consideration, a performance or a return promise must be bargained for.

(2) A performance or return promise is bargained for if it is sought by the promisor in exchange for his promise and is given by the promisee in exchange for that promise.

(3) The performance may consist of

    (a) an act other than a promise, or

    (b) a forbearance, or

    (c) the creation, modification, or destruction of a legal relation.

(4) The performance or return promise may be given to the promisor or to some other person. It may be given by the promisee or by some other person.

### § 209. Integrated Agreements

(1) An integrated agreement is a writing or writings constituting a final expression of one or more terms of an agreement.

(2) Whether there is an integrated agreement is to be determined by the court as a question preliminary to determination of a question of interpretation or to application of the parol evidence rule.

(3) Where the parties reduce an agreement to a writing which in view of its completeness and specificity reasonably appears to be a complete agreement, it is taken to be an integrated agreement unless it is established by other evidence that the writing did not constitute a final expression.

# The Napkin Contract

## Situation

Adam Bernero, a pitcher who split the 2003 season between the Detroit Tigers and the Colorado Rockies, signed his original contract with the Tigers' organization on a napkin at a Denny's Restaurant in Florida. Throughout Bernero's college career at Armstrong Atlantic State University, the Detroit Tigers had kept close tabs on him. Tigers scout Gary York was well aware that other teams were also interested in signing Bernero once his college career ended. For that reason, York hoped to have Bernero sign a Tigers' contract immediately after his last collegiate game. York planned to watch the game, return to his hotel room to pick up his briefcase, and then take Bernero to dinner to obtain his signature on a contract.

Unfortunately for York, Bernero's final college game ended close to midnight. With the formal Tigers' contract back at his hotel, York had to improvise. He followed Bernero and the rest of the Armstrong Atlantic State team to a Denny's Restaurant for a quick post-game meal. At the restaurant, York grabbed a napkin and scribbled out the terms of a basic agreement. The written words stated that "the hereby player, Adam Bernero, agrees to the terms of [Bernero's annual salary] with the Detroit Tigers professional baseball club." Bernero and York both signed the napkin. In this way, Bernero became a Detroit Tiger. A year later, and by then a member of the Tigers' starting rotation, Bernero mused, "It makes me wonder sometimes if it was valid at all. But I am here now so I don't care."

## Issue

Was the napkin a valid medium for purposes of the contract between Adam Bernero and the Detroit Tigers?

## Analysis

Bernero had good reason not to be concerned. Although a napkin is an unorthodox backdrop for a contract, there is nothing to prevent the use of a napkin for this purpose. Any paper or surface on which words can be written and preserved is sufficient. A napkin is not as good a medium as bond paper but, in the end, it is the intent of the parties that governs. So long as the courts are able to decipher the intent of the parties, as demonstrated by written words or other evidence, the material on which agreements are written is of little concern. Bernero's napkin contract sufficed as "a final expression" under § 209 of the Restatement of Contracts.

---

## Sources

Dave Sheinin, "Youth Serves O's with Win," *The Washington Post*, 8 August 2000, D6.

John Lowe, "Scout's Persistence Paid Off with Bernero," *Detroit Free Press*, 8 August 2000.

## References

RESTATEMENT (SECOND) OF CONTRACTS §§ 17, 26, 209 (1981).

### § 17. Requirement of a Bargain

(1) Except as stated in Subsection (2), the formation of a contract requires a bargain in which there is a manifestation of mutual assent to the exchange and a consideration.

(2) Whether or not there is a bargain a contract may be formed under special rules applicable to formal contracts or under the rules stated in §§ 82-94.

### § 26. Preliminary Negotiations

A manifestation of willingness to enter into a bargain is not an offer if the person to whom it is addressed knows or has reason to know that the person making it does not intend to conclude a bargain until he has made a further manifestation of assent.

### § 209. Integrated Agreements

(1) An integrated agreement is a writing or writings constituting a final expression of one or more terms of an agreement.

(2) Whether there is an integrated agreement is to be determined by the court as a question preliminary to determination of a question of interpretation or to application of the parol evidence rule.

(3) Where the parties reduce an agreement to a writing which in view of its completeness and specificity reasonably appears to be a complete agreement, it is taken to be an integrated agreement unless it is established by other evidence that the writing did not constitute a final expression.

# Kitchen Table Contract

## Situation

After receiving a written offer for a contract from the NBA's Washington Bullets for the 1995-96 season, Don MacLean signed the contract. He then left the signed document on his kitchen table. After signing the contract, MacLean told reporters that he had agreed to terms with the Bullets and would practice with the team the following morning. He told John Nash, the Bullets' general manager, the same thing. Nash reminded MacLean that the Bullets hadn't yet received the signed contract back, but MacLean said he would sign the necessary waivers to allow him to practice. Following MacLean's conversation with Nash, the Boston Celtics informed MacLean's agent that they wanted to sign MacLean for the 1995-96 season. The Celtics said they would make an offer to MacLean as soon as they were able to trade veteran point guard Sherman Douglas.

## Issues

Did MacLean's act of signing the Bullets' contract, and then telling general manager John Nash that he had signed the contract, constitute an acceptance of the Bullets' offer?

Did the fact that MacLean's agent engaged in preliminary discussions with the Boston Celtics about a contract, after MacLean had received the Bullets' offer, constitute a rejection of the offer?

## Analysis

The Bullets were apparently of the opinion that MacLean had not accepted the team's offer. Section 30 of the Restatement of Contracts provides that an offeror may require acceptance by performing a specified act. Underlying this principle is the fact that the law considers the offeror to be the master of his offer. Therefore, when accepting an offer, a person must follow the offeror's instructions. In John Nash's view, the terms of acceptance required MacLean to return the signed contract to the Bullets' office. MacLean did not have the option of communicating acceptance through conduct, such as showing up at the team's practice session.

A case could be made that the actions of MacLean's agent amounted to a rejection of the Bullets' offer. Under § 38 of the Restatement of Contracts, a manifestation of an intention not to accept an offer is a rejection unless the offeree indicates an intention to take the offer under further advisement. The fact that the agent spoke with the Boston Celtics while the Bullets' offer was pending may have been a manifestation of MacLean's intent not to accept Washington's offer. In that case, the question of whether there had been an actual rejection of the offer would have depended on whether MacLean or his agent had demonstrated the intent to take the Bullets' offer under further advisement.

## Source

"MacLean Waits for an Offer From Celtics," *The Washington Post*, 7 October 1995, D1–D3.

## References

RESTATEMENT (SECOND) OF CONTRACTS §§ 30, 38 (1981).

### § 30. Form of Acceptance Invited

(1) An offer may invite or require acceptance to be made by an affirmative answer in words, or by performing or refraining from performing a specified act, or may empower the offeree to make a selection of terms in his acceptance.

(2) Unless otherwise indicated by the language or the circumstances, an offer invites acceptance in any manner and by any medium reasonable in the circumstances.

### § 38. Rejection

(1) An offeree's power of acceptance is terminated by his rejection of the offer, unless the offeror has manifested a contrary intention.

(2) A manifestation of intention not to accept an offer is a rejection unless the offeree manifests an intention to take it under further advisement.

# The Dodgers' Blank Player Contracts

## Situation

In the 1950s, when contract negotiations in major league baseball were some-times relatively informal, outfielder Duke Snider and shortstop Pee Wee Reese relied on Dodgers general manager Buzzy Bavasi to fill in salary figures on their player contracts that would be fair compensation. One spring, Snider and Reese both reported unsigned to the Dodgers' Vero Beach, Florida spring training site. As the two Dodger stars prepared to take the field for their first workout, a team official informed them they had to sign player contracts before they could take part in spring training. With that, Bavasi sent over blank contracts for Snider and Reese. They signed the blank contracts and then joined their teammates on the practice field. According to Snider, "We actually didn't know what we were going to be paid until we received our first paycheck."

## Issue

Did the contracts that Snider and Reese signed form valid agreements under the law of contracts?

## Analysis

At common law, for a valid contract to exist, there had to be a "meeting of the minds." The law looked to see if both parties had agreed to the same deal. One can surmise that, when signing the blank contracts, Reese and Snider did not agree to "the same deal" as Buzzy Bavasi because only Bavasi knew how much Reese and Snider would be paid for the season. It is questionable, therefore, whether there really had been a meeting of the minds.

In the modern legal system, however, the common law standard of a meeting of the minds has given way to a more objective test. The law now focuses on whether the parties showed a mutual assent to be bound and whether a reason-able person would find that a contract had been formed. This standard is reflected in §17 of the Restatement of Contracts. For purposes of the Reese and Snider contracts, the modern standard takes a more accommodating and prac-tical stance. Surely, when signing the blank contracts, both Reese and Snider intended to be bound by the contracts and, in effect, to accept the salary levels dictated by the team. The players made a conscious decision to accept whatever salary Bavasi thought to be appropriate. Viewing the transactions from an objective standpoint, one would conclude that Reese and Snider both intended to enter into contracts with the Dodgers.

Under § 33 of the Restatement, the actions of the parties may show conclusively that they intended to conclude a binding agreement, even though one or more of the terms are missing or left to be agreed upon. In such cases, the courts endeavor, if possible, to attach a sufficiently definite meaning to the bargain. This approach is reflected in § 204 of the Restatement. It is obviously an area, however, where the parties should proceed cautiously. The more contractual terms that are left open, the more likely it is that a court would find that the parties lacked the mutual intent to enter into a binding agreement.

## Source

Ron Luciano and David Fisher, *Remembrance of Swings Past* (New York: Bantam Books, 1988), 223.

## References

RESTATEMENT (SECOND) OF CONTRACTS §§ 17, 20, 24, 33, 204 (1981).

### § 17. Requirement of a Bargain

(1) Except as stated in Subsection (2), the formation of a contract requires a bargain in which there is a manifestation of mutual assent to the exchange and a consideration.

(2) Whether or not there is a bargain a contract may be formed under special rules applicable to formal contracts or under the rules stated in §§ 82-94.

### § 20. Effect of Misunderstanding

(1) There is no manifestation of mutual assent to an exchange if the parties attach materially different meanings to their manifestations and (a) neither party knows or has reason to know the meaning attached by the other; or (b) each party knows or each party has reason to know the meaning attached by the other.

(2) The manifestations of the parties are operative in accordance with the meaning attached to them by one of the parties if (a) that party does not know of any different meaning attached by the other; and the other knows the meaning attached by the first party; or (b) that party has no reason to know of any different meaning attached by the other, and the other has reason to know the meaning attached by the first party.

## § 24. Offer Defined

An offer is the manifestation of willingness to enter into a bargain, so made as to justify another person in understanding that his assent to that bargain is invited and will conclude it.

## § 33. Certainty

(1) Even though a manifestation of intention is intended to be understood as an offer, it cannot be accepted so as to form a contract unless the terms of the contract are reasonably certain.

(2) The terms of a contract are reasonably certain if they provide a basis for determining the existence of a breach and for giving an appropriate remedy.

(3) The fact that one or more terms of a proposed bargain are left open or uncertain may show that a manifestation of intention is not intended to be understood as an offer or as an acceptance.

## § 204. Supplying an Omitted Essential Term

When the parties to a bargain sufficiently defined to be a contract have not agreed with respect to a term which is essential to a determination of their rights and duties, a term which is reasonable in the circumstances is supplied by the court.

# *Avoiding a Contract*

## Major League Misrepresentation

### Situation

For much of his ten-year major league career, pitcher Bob Locker was one of the most successful relief pitchers in the American League. He also had one remarkable season, 1967, in which he saved 20 games, won 7 more, limited opposing teams to 2.09 earned runs per nine innings, and struck out nearly four times as many batters as he walked. Locker's exceptional season came one year after fellow pitcher Phil Regan had enjoyed an even more spectacular year for the Los Angeles Dodgers. Regan had won fourteen games in relief for the Dodgers in 1966 and lost only one. He led the National League with 21 saves and recorded a 1.62 earned run average.

After his exceptional performance in 1967, Locker asked the White Sox for a raise to $18,000. The White Sox countered with an offer of $16,000. White Sox general manager Ed Short supported his counter-offer by referring to Phil Regan's salary. Short told Locker that his demand was out of line because Regan had just signed with the Dodgers for $23,000. Locker said to Short, "if Regan is making only $23,000, then I'm asking too much. You check that. If he signed for $23,000, I'll sign for $16,000." The next day Short called Locker and said, "I called Buzzy Bavasi (then general manager of the Dodgers), and he told me Regan was making $23,000 this year." Locker proceeded to sign his 1968 contract for $16,000. After signing his contract, Locker wrote Regan a letter "just for the hell of it." Locker asked Regan if he would mind telling him how much he was making. Regan wrote back saying that he had signed for $36,500.

### Issue

Did Bob Locker have a legal basis for avoiding his contract with the Chicago White Sox?

### Analysis

The negotiations between Ed Short and Bob Locker form a classic case of misrepresentation and reliance. Section 162 of the Restatement of Contracts and § 526 of the Restatement of Torts leave no doubt that the misrepresentation was fraudulent. To establish fraudulent misrepresentation, § 162 would require a showing that Short: (1) intended to induce Locker to rely on his assertion regarding Regan's salary, and (2) either knew his assertion was not true or lacked a basis for the assertion.

Locker was justified in relying on Short's assurances. He accepted a salary of $16,000 based on those assurances. Accordingly, § 164 of the Restatement of Contracts would permit Locker to avoid the contract. Under § 380(2) of the Restatement of Contracts, however, Locker would have had only a limited period of time in which to avoid the contract. Once Locker suited up for the White Sox and took the mound after having received Phil Regan's letter, his actions had the effect of affirming his acceptance of the $16,000 salary.

## Source

Jim Bouton, *Ball Four: My Life and Hard Times Throwing the Knuckleball in the Big Leagues* (Cleveland, Ohio: The World Publishing Company, 1970), 212.

## References

• RESTATEMENT (SECOND) OF CONTRACTS §§ 159, 162, 164, 376, 380 (1981).

§ 159. Misrepresentation Defined

A misrepresentation is an assertion that is not in accord with the facts.

§ 162. When a Misrepresentation Is Fraudulent or Material

(1) A misrepresentation is fraudulent if the maker intends his assertion to induce a party to manifest his assent and the maker:

    (a)   knows or believes that the assertion is not in accord with the facts, or

    (b)   does not have the confidence that he states or implies in the truth of the assertion, or

    (c)   knows that he does not have the basis that he states or implies for the assertion.

(2) A misrepresentation is material if it would be likely to induce a reasonable person to manifest his assent, or if the maker knows that it would be likely to induce the recipient to do so.

### § 164. When a Misrepresentation Makes a Contract Voidable

(1) If a party's manifestation of assent is induced by either a fraudulent or a material misrepresentation by the other party upon which the recipient is justified in relying, the contract is voidable by the recipient.

(2) If a party's manifestation of assent is induced by either a fraudulent or a material misrepresentation by one who is not a party to the transaction upon which the recipient is justified in relying, the contract is voidable by the recipient, unless the other party to the transaction in good faith and without reason to know of the misrepresentation either gives value or relies materially on the transaction.

### § 376. Restitution When Contract Is Voidable

A party who has avoided a contract on the ground of lack of capacity, mistake, misrepresentation, duress, undue influence or abuse of a fiduciary relationship is entitled to restitution for any benefit that he has conferred on the other party by way of part performance or reliance.

### § 380. Loss of Power of Avoidance by Affirmance

(1) The power of a party to avoid a contract for incapacity, duress, undue influence or abuse of a fiduciary relationship is lost if, after the circumstances that made the contract voidable have ceased to exist, he manifests to the other party his intention to affirm it or acts with respect to anything that he has received in a manner inconsistent with disaffirmance.

(2) The power of a party to avoid a contract for mistake or misrepresentation is lost if after he knows or has reason to know of the mistake or misrepresentation if it is nonfraudulent or knows of the misrepresentation if it is fraudulent, he manifests to the other party his intention to affirm it or acts with respect to anything that he has received in a manner inconsistent with disaffirmance.

(3) If the other party rejects an offer by the party seeking avoidance to return what he has received, the party seeking avoidance if entitled to restitution can, after the lapse of reasonable time, enforce a lien on what he has received by selling it and crediting the proceeds toward his claim in restitution.

• RESTATEMENT (SECOND) OF TORTS §§ 525, 526, 531, 537, 538 (1965).

### § 525. Liability for Fraudulent Misrepresentation

One who fraudulently makes a misrepresentation of fact, opinion, intention or law for the purpose of inducing another to act or to refrain from action in reliance upon it, is subject to liability to the other in deceit for pecuniary loss caused to him by his justifiable reliance upon the misrepresentation.

## § 526. Conditions Under Which Misrepresentation Is Fraudulent

A misrepresentation is fraudulent if the maker

- (a) knows or believes that the matter is not as he represents it to be,
- (b) does not have the confidence in the accuracy of his representation that he states or implies, or
- (c) knows that he does not have the basis for his representation that he states or implies.

## § 531. General Rule [Liability for Fraudulent Misrepresentation]

One who makes a fraudulent misrepresentation is subject to liability to the persons or class of persons whom he intends or has reason to expect to act or to refrain from action in reliance upon the misrepresentation, for pecuniary loss suffered by them through their justifiable reliance in the type of transaction in which he intends or has reason to expect their conduct to be influenced.

## § 537. General Rule [Recovery for Fraudulent Misrepresentation]

The recipient of a fraudulent misrepresentation can recover against its maker for pecuniary loss resulting from it if, but only if,

- (a) he relies on the misrepresentation in acting or refraining from action, and
- (b) his reliance is justifiable.

## § 538. Materiality of Misrepresentation

(1) Reliance upon a fraudulent misrepresentation is not justifiable unless the matter misrepresented is material.

(2) The matter is material if

- (a) a reasonable man would attach importance to its existence or nonexistence in determining his choice of action in the transaction in question; or
- (b) the maker of the misrepresentation knows or has reason to know that its recipient regards or is likely to regard the matter as important in determining his choice of action, although a reasonable man would not so regard it.

# *Breach of Contract*

## A Month of Rap

### Situation

Seeking to establish a niche as a rap star, Indiana Pacers forward Ron Artest asked the Pacers' coach, Rick Carlisle, for a month off from basketball at the start of the 2004-2005 National Basketball Association season. According to Artest, the purpose of the proposed "sabbatical" was to allow some time for him to promote his debut rap album. Carlisle was not amused. In his view, Artest's request "compromised the integrity of the team." Artest seemed not to understand. "They probably expected a little more; expected me to play in every game," he said. "It's early in the season, so I feel like I could take some time off early and be ready for the long stretch."

### Issues

If Artest had taken time off from basketball, without approval from the Pacers, would his actions have been a material breach of contract?

Would the Pacers have been able to seek monetary damages from Artest for total breach of his contract?

### Analysis

Under § 241 of the Restatement of Contracts, the determination as to whether Artest's breach would be material would depend primarily on three factors: (1) the extent to which the Pacers would be deprived of Artest's contributions; (2) the compensation available to the Pacers, if any, for the financial loss arising from Artest's absence; and (3) the extent to which Artest's conduct fell short of the requirement for fair dealing. It seems likely that, under § 241, an unauthorized absence for 30 days would have been a material breach.

The Pacers would look to § 243 of the Restatement of Contracts for guidance on whether Artest's breach gave rise to a claim for damages for total breach of his contract. Under § 243(4), the Pacers would not be entitled to damages for a total breach. Though Rick Carlisle might be inclined to disagree, Artest's absence for a month would not have substantially impaired the long-term value that the Pacers could expect to derive from Artest's contract.

## Source

"Artest Benched for Asking Carlisle for Time Off," www.cbs.sportsline.com, 10 November 2004.

## References

RESTATEMENT (SECOND) OF CONTRACTS §§ 89, 205, 235, 241, 243 (1981).

### § 89. Modification of Executory Contract

A promise modifying a duty under a contract not fully performed on either side is binding:

(a)  if the modification is fair and equitable in view of circumstances not anticipated by the parties when the contract was made; or

(b)  to the extent provided by statute; or

(c)  to the extent that justice requires enforcement in view of material change of position in reliance on the promise.

### § 205. Duty of Good Faith and Fair Dealing

Every contract imposes upon each party a duty of good faith and fair dealing in its performance and its enforcement.

### § 235. Effect of Performance as Discharge and of Non-Performance as Breach

(1)  Full performance of a duty under a contract discharges the duty.

(2)  When performance of a duty under a contract is due any non-performance is a breach.

### § 241. Circumstances Significant in Determining Whether a Failure Is Material

In determining whether a failure to render or to offer performance is material, the following circumstances are significant:

(a)  the extent to which the injured party will be deprived of the benefit which he reasonably expected;

(b)  the extent to which the injured party can be adequately compensated for the part of that benefit of which he will be deprived;

(c)  the extent to which the party failing to perform or to offer to perform will suffer forfeiture;

(d) the likelihood that the party failing to perform or to offer to perform will cure his failure, taking into account of all the circumstances including any reasonable assurances;

(e) the extent to which the behavior of the party failing to perform or to offer to perform comports with standards of good faith and fair dealing.

## § 243. Effect of a Breach by Non-performance as Giving Rise to a Claim for Damages for Total Breach

(1) With respect to performances to be exchanged under an exchange of promises, a breach by non-performance gives rise to a claim for damages for total breach only if it discharges the injured party's remaining duties to render such performance, other than a duty to render an agreed equivalent under § 240.

(2) Except as stated in Subsection (3), a breach by nonperformance accompanied or followed by a repudiation gives rise to a claim for damages for total breach.

(3) Where at the time of the breach the only remaining duties of performance are those of the party in breach and are for the payment of money in installments not related to one another, his breach by non-performance as to less than the whole, whether or not accompanied or followed by a repudiation, does not give rise to a claim for damages for total breach.

(4) In any case other than those stated in the preceding subsections, a breach by non-performance gives rise to a claim for total breach only if it so substantially impairs the value of the contract to the injured party at the time of the breach that it is just in the circumstances to allow him to recover damages based on all his remaining rights to performance.

# Enforcement of Contracts

## The Fantastic Dr. J Leaves Town

### Situation

Led by the exploits of Julius Erving, known to basketball fans as "Dr. J," the New York Nets captured the American Basketball Association championship during the 1975-1976 season. The next season the Nets joined the National Basketball Association. To promote sales of season tickets, the Nets structured an advertising campaign around Erving. The ads read, "See the fantastic Dr. 'J' in action." Notwithstanding the team's advertisements touting Dr. J, the Nets sold the all-star to the Philadelphia 76ers at the start of the 1976-1977 season. A disgruntled fan sued the Nets. The fan argued that he had entered into a contract with the New York Nets, paying money in exchange for the right to see Dr. J play basketball. In the fan's view, by trading Erving to the 76ers, the Nets breached the team's duty under the contract entered into when the fan purchased his season tickets.

### Issue

Under the law of contracts, did the New York Nets have a contractual duty to allow season-ticket holders to watch the fantastic Dr. 'J' in action?

### Analysis

The lawsuit alleged that, with the trade of Dr. J, the "product" that the season-ticket holder purchased no longer existed. The season-ticket holder argued that his contract for purchase of a season ticket was frustrated. Section 265 of the Restatement of Contracts governs frustration of contract. To successfully assert frustration of contract, the fan would have had to demonstrate that: (1) watching Dr. J play was his principal purpose in buying a season ticket; (2) the continued presence of Dr. J on the Nets' roster was a basic assumption underlying his purchase; and (3) the frustration of contract resulting from the trade of Dr. J was so severe that it was not within the realm of risks that ticket buyers usually assume. The judge sided with the Nets. The decision in *Strauss v. Long Island Sports, Inc.* states that it is unreasonable for any fan to presume there will be no player trades. According to the judge, the possible trade of Dr. J or any other Nets player was among the risks that ticket holders routinely assumed. There was, the judge found, no frustration of contract.

---

## Source

*Strauss v. Long Island Sports, Inc., doing business as the New York Nets*, 401 N.Y. Supp. 2d 223 (1978).

## References

RESTATEMENT (SECOND) OF CONTRACTS §§ 4, 5, 265, 317 (1981).

### § 4. How a Promise May Be Made

A promise may be stated in words either oral or written, or may be inferred wholly or partly from conduct.

### § 5. Terms of Promise, Agreement or Contract

(1) A term of a promise or agreement is that portion of the intention or assent manifested which relates to a particular matter.

(2) A term of a contract is that portion of the legal relations resulting from the promise or set of promises which relates to a particular matter, whether or not the parties manifest an intention to create those relations.

### § 265. Discharge by Supervening Frustration

Where, after a contract is made, a party's principal purpose is substantially frustrated without his fault by the occurrence of an event the non-occurrence of which was a basic assumption on which the contract was made, his remaining duties to render performance are discharged, unless the language or the circumstances indicate the contrary.

### § 317. Assignment of a Right

(1) An assignment of a right is a manifestation of the assignor's intention to transfer it by virtue of which the assignor's right to performance by the obligor is extinguished in whole or in part and the assignee acquires a right to such performance.

(2) A contractual right can be assigned unless:

    (a) the substitution of a right of the assignee for the right of the assignor would materially change the duty of the obligor, or materially increase the burden or risk imposed on him by his contract, or materially impair his chance of obtaining return performance, or materially reduce its value to him, or

(b)  the assignment is forbidden by statute or is otherwise inoperative on grounds of public policy, or

(c)  assignment is validly precluded by contract.

# No Flowers for New York

## Situation

In 1960, Charlie Flowers, a standout running back from the University of Mississippi, signed a contract to play with the Los Angeles Chargers of the American Football League after he had already agreed to a two-year deal with the National Football League's New York Giants. The Giants had signed Flowers to a contract before the 1960 Sugar Bowl, in which the University of Mississippi was scheduled to play. By signing with the Giants, Flowers became a professional and, under collegiate rules, no longer eligible to play in the Sugar Bowl. However, the Giants agreed to keep Flowers' contract secret until after the Sugar Bowl. The subterfuge was designed to allow Flowers to participate in the bowl game. In the days leading up to the Sugar Bowl, the Chargers offered Flowers a contract that would pay him more money than his agreement with the Giants. After the Sugar Bowl, Flowers returned his signing bonus to the Giants and signed with Los Angeles. In an effort to keep Flowers in New York's royal blue uniform, the Giants took the Chargers to court.

## Issue

Under the law, which team would hold the rights to the services of Charlie Flowers?

## Analysis

The case went to trial and was ultimately heard, on appeal, by the U.S. Court of Appeals for the Fifth Circuit. In a harshly worded opinion, the Court of Appeals found the Giants guilty of "devious and deceitful conduct." The Court of Appeals also criticized the trial court for not dismissing the Giants' lawsuit on the basis of the "clean hands" doctrine. No party, the court stated, has the right to foist a pretended status on the public and then approach the judicial system as if it had acted in good faith. The Giants had "soiled their hands," the court declared, by signing Flowers before the Sugar Bowl and then concealing the contract. The court ruled that Flowers was free to play for the Chargers.

The "clean hands" doctrine is derived from the unwillingness of a court to give relief to a suitor who has conducted himself in a way that shocks the moral sensibilities of the court. The doctrine is not a response, in any way, to the relative rights and liabilities of the parties under the law of contracts. Rather, it is a reflection of conduct by the plaintiff that the court, as a matter of public policy, finds unseemly. The public policy interest in requiring plaintiffs to come to the court with "clean hands" is reflected in § 178 of the Restatement of Contracts.

## Source

*New York Football Giants, Inc. v. Los Angeles Chargers Football Club, Inc.*, 291 F.2d 471 (5th Circuit 1961).

## References

RESTATEMENT (SECOND) OF CONTRACTS §§ 1, 178, 179 (1981).

### § 1. Contract Defined

A contract is a promise or a set of promises for the breach of which the law gives a remedy, or the performance of which the law in some way recognizes as a duty.

### § 178. When a Term Is Unenforceable on Grounds of Public Policy

(1) A promise or other term of an agreement is unenforceable on grounds of public policy if legislation provides that it is unenforceable or the interest in its enforcement is clearly outweighed in the circumstances by a public policy against the enforcement of such terms.

(2) In weighing the interest in the enforcement of a term, account is taken of

    (a) the parties' justified expectations,

    (b) any forfeiture that would result if enforcement were denied, and

    (c) any special public interest in the enforcement of the particular term.

(3) In weighing a public policy against enforcement of a term, account is taken of

    (a) the strength of that policy as manifested by legislation or judicial decisions,

    (b) the likelihood that a refusal to enforce the term will further that policy,

    (c) the seriousness of any misconduct involved and the extent to which it was deliberate, and

    (d) the directness of the connection between that misconduct and the term.

### § 179. Bases of Public Policies Against Enforcement

A public policy against the enforcement of promises or other terms may be derived by the court from

    (a) legislation relevant to such a policy, or

(b) the need to protect some aspect of the public welfare, as is the case for the judicial policies against, for example,

(i) restraint of trade (§§ 186-188),

(ii) impairment of family relations (§§ 189-191), and

(iii) interference with other protected interests (§§ 192-196, 356).

# Boston-Bound

## Situation

Danny Ainge, a two-sport star at Brigham Young University, signed a contract to play baseball for the Toronto Blue Jays after completing his college career. Ainge, an infielder and outfielder, played for the Blue Jays from 1979 to 1981. In those three years, however, he was unable to adjust to big league pitching, hitting a collective .220. The experience soured Ainge on major league baseball. He told the Blue Jays that he wanted to pursue a career in basketball. The Boston Celtics held the draft rights to Ainge and looked forward to adding him to their roster. Even though he was still under contract with the Blue Jays, Ainge signed to play for the Celtics. The Blue Jays sued the Celtics to enforce their contractual rights to Ainge.

## Issue

Under the law of contracts, did the Toronto Blue Jays have a valid legal basis for preventing Danny Ainge from playing basketball for the Boston Celtics?

## Analysis

The court found that Ainge's contract with the Blue Jays prevented him from becoming a professional basketball player until he had fulfilled his baseball contract. The court's decision was consistent with the principle set forth in § 235 of the Restatement of Contracts, which states that the failure to perform a contractual obligation, when that obligation is due, is a breach. In his decision, the judge noted that Ainge would have been free to accept a job as a non-playing college basketball coach or other jobs that did not involve the playing of a professional sport.

After the judge issued his decision, the Blue Jays revealed that the team's objective was simply to establish that Ainge was contractually obligated to Toronto. Having prevailed in court, the Blue Jays gave up their rights to Ainge and released him from his contract, reportedly in exchange for a $500,000 payment from the Celtics.

## Source

*Toronto Blue Jays Baseball Club v. Boston Celtics Corp.*, No. 81-5263 (S.D.N.Y. October 19, 1981).

## References

RESTATEMENT (SECOND) OF CONTRACTS §§ 1, 2, 205, 235, 344, 345, 347 (1981).

### § 1. Contract Defined

A contract is a promise or a set of promises for the breach of which the law gives a remedy, or the performance of which the law in some way recognizes as a duty.

### § 2. Promise; Promisor; Promisee; Beneficiary

(1) A promise is a manifestation of intention to act or refrain from acting in a specified way, so made as to justify a promisee in understanding that a commitment has been made.

(2) The person manifesting the intention is the promisor.

(3) The person to whom the manifestation is addressed is the promisee.

(4) Where performance will benefit a person other than the promisee, that person is a beneficiary.

### § 205. Duty of Good Faith and Fair Dealing

Every contract imposes upon each party a duty of good faith and fair dealing in its performance and its enforcement.

### § 235. Effect of Performance as Discharge and of Non-Performance as Breach

(1) Full performance of a duty under a contract discharges the duty.

(2) When performance of a duty under a contract is due any non-performance is a breach.

### § 344. Purposes of Remedies

Judicial remedies under the rules stated in this Restatement serve to protect one or more of the following interests of a promisee:

(a) his "expectation interest," which is his interest in having the benefit of his bargain by being put in as good a position as he would have been in had the contract been performed,

(b) his "reliance interest," which is his interest in being reimbursed for loss caused by reliance on the contract by being put in as good a position as he would have been in had the contract not been made, or

(c) his "restitution interest," which is his interest in having restored to him any benefit that he has conferred on the other party.

## § 345. Judicial Remedies Available

The judicial remedies available for the protection of the interests stated in § 344 include a judgment or order

(a) awarding a sum of money due under the contract or as damages,

(b) requiring specific performance of a contract or enjoining its non-performance,

(c) requiring restoration of a specific thing to prevent unjust enrichment,

(d) awarding a sum of money to prevent unjust enrichment,

(e) declaring the rights of the parties, and

(f) enforcing an arbitration award.

## § 347. Measure of Damages in General

Subject to the limitations stated in §§ 350-53, the injured party has a right to damages based on his expectation interest as measured by

(a) the loss in the value to him of the other party's performance caused by its failure or deficiency, plus

(b) any other loss, including incidental or consequential loss, caused by the breach, less

(c) any cost or other loss that he has avoided by not having to perform.

# The Ill-Fated Incentive Clause

## Situation

Basketball player Paul Westphal's 1983-84 contract with the Phoenix Suns contained an incentive clause that guaranteed Westphal an extra $250,000 if he played in at least 60 games during the season. As it turned out, Westphal played in only 59 games. There were two games in which Westphal's playing stats read "DNP-Coach's Decision." For reasons unknown, coach John MacLeod had held Westphal out of two games in which he was available to play. Westphal sued the Suns for breach of contract.

## Issue

Under the law of contracts, were the Phoenix Suns obligated to pay Paul Westphal the $250,000 bonus specified in his contract?

## Analysis

Westphal believed the Suns had acted in bad faith. Under § 205 of the Restatement of Contracts, the team had an obligation to act fairly. Yet, the court was reluctant to read into the contract a term to which the parties had not agreed. From the court's perspective, both the literal words of the contract and the parties' intent were clear: Westphal had to play in 60 games to earn the bonus. The court ruled in favor of the Suns.

In the opinion of long-time Boston Celtics coach and general manager Red Auerbach, the judge reached the proper decision. Auerbach felt that the Suns had outsmarted Westphal and his agent. In Auerbach's view, "if they had worded the perk correctly—specifying how many games Paul was *available* to play in, rather than how many games he actually played—they would have been able to pocket the dough." Section 20 of the Restatement of Contracts reflects Auerbach's view. Westphal assented to the literal words contained in the bonus clause. The Suns would have had no way of knowing that Westphal and his agent interpreted the clause as requiring payment if Westphal was available to play in 60 games but actually played in less than 60.

## Source

Red Auerbach with Joe Fitzgerald, *On and Off the Court* (New York: Bantam Books, 1986), 98.

## References

RESTATEMENT (SECOND) OF CONTRACTS §§ 1, 20, 71, 204, 205 (1981).

### § 1. Contract Defined

A contract is a promise or a set of promises for the breach of which the law gives a remedy, or the performance of which the law in some way recognizes as a duty.

### § 20. Effect of Misunderstanding

(1) There is no manifestation of mutual assent to an exchange if the parties attach materially different meanings to their manifestations and

(a) neither party knows or has reason to know the meaning attached by the other; or

(b) each party knows or each party has reason to know the meaning attached by the other.

(2) The manifestations of the parties are operative in accordance with the meaning attached to them by one of the parties if

(a) that party does not know of any different meaning attached by the other; and the other knows the meaning attached by the first party; or

(b) that party has no reason to know of any different meaning attached by the other, and the other has reason to know the meaning attached by the first party.

### § 71. Requirement of Exchange; Types of Exchange

(1) To constitute consideration, a performance or a return promise must be bargained for.

(2) A performance or return promise is bargained for if it is sought by the promisor in exchange for his promise and is given by the promisee in exchange for that promise.

(3) The performance may consist of

(a) an act other than a promise, or

(b) a forbearance, or

(c) the creation, modification, or destruction of a legal relation.

(4) The performance or return promise may be given to the promisor or to some other person. It may be given by the promisee or by some other person.

## § 204. Supplying an Omitted Essential Term

When the parties to a bargain sufficiently defined to be a contract have not agreed with respect to a term which is essential to a determination of their rights and duties, a term which is reasonable in the circumstances is supplied by the court.

## § 205. Duty of Good Faith and Fair Dealing

Every contract imposes upon each party a duty of good faith and fair dealing in its performance and its enforcement.

# The Fighing (sic) Irish

## Situation

In 1995, a 22-year-old fan of the University of Notre Dame football team contracted with a Carlstadt, New Jersey tattoo parlor to have the words "Fighting Irish" inscribed in a tattoo on his arm. Upon completion of the job, the Notre Dame fan discovered to his dismay that the tattoo artist had left out the "t" in "Fighting." The inscription read, "Fighing Irish." The fan sued the tattoo parlor for damages.

## Issue

Did the Notre Dame fan have a basis under the law of contracts for suing the tattoo parlor?

## Analysis

The Notre Dame fan contracted to have "Fighting" spelled with eight characters. The tattoo artist's work fell one character short. The failure to provide the requisite "t" would be a breach of contract under § 235 of the Restatement of Contracts. The spelling error would likely constitute a material breach under § 241 of the Restatement as well. At least two of the circumstances identified in § 241 as suggesting a material breach are applicable: the fan clearly was deprived of the benefit which he reasonably expected, and the unique nature of the breach likely made it impossible to effect any kind of cure.

---

## Source

"Dye-Hard Fan," *The Washington Post*, 1 January 1996, C3.

## References

RESTATEMENT (SECOND) OF CONTRACTS §§ 89, 233, 235, 241 (1981).

### § 89. Modification of Executory Contract

A promise modifying a duty under a contract not fully performed on either side is binding:

(a) if the modification is fair and equitable in view of circumstances not anticipated by the parties when the contract was made; or

(b) to the extent provided by statute; or

(c) to the extent that justice requires enforcement in view of material change of position in reliance on the promise.

## § 233. Performance at One Time or in Installments

(1) Where performances are to be exchanged under an exchange of promises, and the whole of one party's performance can be rendered at one time, it is due at one time, unless the language or the circumstances indicate the contrary.

(2) Where only a part of one party's performance is due at one time under Subsection (1), if the other party's performance can be so apportioned that there is a comparable part that can also be rendered at that time, it is due at that time, unless the language or the circumstances indicate the contrary.

## § 235. Effect of Performance as Discharge and of Non-Performance as Breach

(1) Full performance of a duty under a contract discharges the duty.

(2) When performance of a duty under a contract is due any non-performance is a breach.

## § 241. Circumstances Significant in Determining Whether a Failure Is Material

In determining whether a failure to render or to offer performance is material, the following circumstances are significant:

(a) the extent to which the injured party will be deprived of the benefit which he reasonably expected;

(b) the extent to which the injured party can be adequately compensated for the part of that benefit of which he will be deprived;

(c) the extent to which the party failing to perform or to offer to perform will suffer forfeiture;

(d) the likelihood that the party failing to perform or to offer to perform will cure his failure, taking into account of all the circumstances including any reasonable assurances;

(e) the extent to which the behavior of the party failing to perform or to offer to perform comports with standards of good faith and fair dealing.

# The Misplaced Tickets

## Situation

In a twist on the traditional notion of duty of care, a New York Jets football fan once sued the team after he had lost his season tickets for the Jets' home games. The fan had purchased season tickets for three seats during the 1989-1990 season. When the fan discovered that he had lost his tickets, he asked the Jets to issue replacement tickets. The team refused. However, team officials told the fan that if he again paid the face value of the tickets, they would give him tickets for the same seats. The Jets also advised the fan that if the original tickets turned up later, the team would issue a refund. The fan paid again for two of the season tickets and then sued the Jets for double billing and unjust enrichment.

## Issue

Under the law of contracts, were the Jets within their rights when they required the fan to pay the full cost of the replacement tickets?

## Analysis

The court ruled in favor of the Jets. The court held that, to fulfill the terms of his contract with the Jets, the fan had to satisfy the condition of presenting the tickets when entering the stadium. With respect to the lost tickets, the fan was unable to fulfill the condition. The court's analysis is consistent with § 58 of the Restatement of Contracts. Under § 58, the purchaser of season tickets is in the position of offeree and must necessarily render the performance demanded by the offeror, *i.e.*, present the tickets in order to gain admission to the games. In the court's analysis, the fan was obligated to take care of his tickets. He failed in that obligation. The court noted that, in the past, there had been instances where fans had lied about losing their tickets in an effort to get extra tickets without charge. In light of the Jets' prior experiences, the court found that the team's policy regarding the replacement of lost tickets was a necessary precaution to ensure the safety and well-being of fans during games.

## Source

*Ganey v. New York Jets Football Club*, 550 N.Y.S.2d 566 (N.Y. City Civ. Ct. 1990).

## References

Restatement (Second) of Contracts §§ 58, 224, 225 (1981).

### § 58. Necessity of Acceptance Complying With Terms of Offer

An acceptance must comply with the requirements of the offer as to the promise to be made or the performance to be rendered.

### § 224. Condition Defined

A condition is an event, not certain to occur, which must occur, unless its non-occurrence is excused, before performance under a contract becomes due.

### § 225. Effects of the Non-occurrence of a Condition

(1) Performance of a duty subject to a condition cannot become due unless the condition occurs or its non-occurrence is excused.

(2) Unless it has been excused, the non-occurrence of a condition discharges the duty when the condition can no longer occur.

(3) Non-occurrence of a condition is not a breach by a party unless he is under a duty that the condition occur.

# *Trading Places*

## <u>Baseballs By The Dozen</u>

### <u>Situation</u>

During his three years in the major leagues, pitcher Tim Fortugno won 3 games and lost 4, with an earned run average of 5.06. Fortugno's professional career, which began in 1986, was notable primarily because he was always on the move. In the period from 1986 to 1995, Fortugno played for sixteen different teams. At one time or another, he was the "property" of seven different major league organizations. For Fortugno, being traded was a way of life. Even so, it was probably a bit unsettling to him when he learned the details of his trade, in 1989, to the Milwaukee Brewers. At the time of the trade, Fortugno was playing for the Reno (Nevada) Silver Sox. The Silver Sox traded him to the Brewers in exchange for twelve dozen baseballs and $2,500.

There is no question that the Milwaukee Brewers had the right to trade or give away twelve dozen baseballs—provided, of course, that they owned the baseballs. The trading of players, however, involves different principles.

### <u>Issue</u>

What is the legal basis for the trading of players in professional sports?

### <u>Analysis</u>

Trades involving professional athletes are based on principles of contract. Whether the sport is baseball, basketball, football or hockey, any player trade starts with the contracts that have been signed with the player or players involved in the trade. Teams can trade a player only if they have bargained for that right, as reflected in the terms of the contract. The wording from the National Football League's standard player contract is representative. The standard NFL contract states "Unless this contract specifically provides otherwise, Club may assign this contract and Player's services under this contract to any successor to Club's franchise or to any other Club in the League." From a legal perspective, a trade involves two parallel actions: (1) the team holding the contractual rights to a player's performance assigns those rights to another team for the agreed-upon value or consideration, and (2) the player's former team delegates to the new team the duty to pay the player's salary. For purposes of the Restatement of Contracts, player trades have their basis in § 317 governing the assignment of contractual rights and § 318 governing the delegation of contractual duties.

## Source

Tim Kurkjian, "Swing Shift," *Sports Illustrated*, 23 January 1995, 70, 74.

## References

RESTATEMENT (SECOND) OF CONTRACTS §§ 317, 318 (1981).

### § 317. Assignment of a Right

(1) An assignment of a right is a manifestation of the assignor's intention to transfer it by virtue of which the assignor's right to performance by the obligor is extinguished in whole or in part and the assignee acquires a right to such performance.

(2) A contractual right can be assigned unless:

    (a) the substitution of a right of the assignee for the right of the assignor would materially change the duty of the obligor, or materially increase the burden or risk imposed on him by his contract, or materially impair his chance of obtaining return performance, or materially reduce its value to him, or

    (b) the assignment is forbidden by statute or is otherwise inoperative on grounds of public policy, or

    (c) assignment is validly precluded by contract.

### § 318. Delegation of Performance of Duty

(1) An obligor can properly delegate the performance of his duty to another unless the delegation is contrary to public policy or the terms of his promise.

(2) Unless otherwise agreed, a promise requires performance by a particular person only to the extent that the obligee has a substantial interest in having that person perform or control the acts promised.

(3) Unless the obligee agrees otherwise, neither delegation of performance nor a contract to assume the duty made with the obligor by the person delegated discharges any duty or liability of the delegating obligor.

# Three-Way Trade

## Situation

In February 2001, Chicago Cubs fans nearly lost Slammin' Sammy Sosa to a three-way deal. The Cubs had all but completed a three-way trade with the Los Angeles Dodgers and the New York Mets involving Sosa. The proposed trade would have sent Sosa to Los Angeles. In turn, the Dodgers would have sent outfielder Gary Sheffield to the New York Mets. As the final leg of the three-way trade, the Mets had agreed to send some of their top minor league prospects to the Cubs. However, the three teams never finalized the deal. Sosa was a veteran of more than ten years in the major leagues and had spent more than five years with the Cubs. As a "ten-and-five" veteran, Sosa had earned the right, under baseball's Collective Bargaining Agreement, to veto any proposed trade with which he was not in agreement. Sosa vetoed the three-way trade and was thereby able to continue playing in the friendly confines of Chicago's Wrigley Field.

## Issue

Is a three-way trade permissible under the law of contracts?

## Analysis

Three-way trades are not as common in sports as two-way trades, but there is nothing to prohibit a three-way trade such as the one that nearly sent Sammy Sosa to the Dodgers. The Restatement of Contracts, § 9, requires that there be at least two parties, a promisor and a promisee, for every contract. However, § 9 also specifically provides that there may be more than two parties. Clearly, therefore, a three-way trade is permissible.

---

## Source

"Sammy Sosa Blocks Three-Way Trade," www.latinosportslegends.com, 22 February 2001.

## Reference

RESTATEMENT (SECOND) OF CONTRACTS § 9 (1981).

## § 9. Parties Required

There must be at least two parties to a contract, a promisor and a promise, but there may be any greater number.

# Tempting Cuisine

## Situation

When first baseman Fred McGriff played for the Tampa Bay Devil Rays during the years from 1998 to 2001, his contract contained a "no-trade" clause prohibiting the Devil Rays from trading him for the duration of the agreement. In the event the Devil Rays wanted to trade McGriff, they would have had to persuade him to waive his no-trade clause. On July 8, 2001, the Devil Rays worked out a tentative deal that would have sent McGriff to the Chicago Cubs. The Cubs, positioning themselves for the pennant race, were in need of a power hitter to bat behind Sammy Sosa. McGriff seemed to be a perfect fit. To the Cubs' dismay, however, McGriff was not anxious to change teams. After consulting with his family, McGriff exercised his rights under his no-trade clause and nixed the deal. As baseball commentator Joe Morgan would say later, though, it was a "soft no."

Less than a month after McGriff declined the trade to Chicago, the Devil Rays again approached him about waiving his no-trade provision. This time, McGriff was more receptive. Two days later, McGriff was in a Cubs uniform and playing first base for his new team in a nationally televised game against the St. Louis Cardinals. In an interview played during the telecast, McGriff explained his reasons for waiving his no-trade clause. His family was supportive, he said, and he felt he would be better able to control his career options in Chicago. To top it off, McGriff said, Chicago was home to "Ron of Japan," his favorite Japanese restaurant.

## Issue

What is the legal basis for "no-trade" clauses in the contracts of professional athletes?

## Analysis

As noted previously, the legal basis for player trades is set forth in § 317 and § 318 of the Restatement of Contracts. The principle articulated in § 317 enables a team to assign a player's contract to another team unless the assignment changes the duties of the player, increases the risk or burden to the player, or is validly precluded by contract. When a player with a no-trade clause objects to a trade, the player is asserting his rights under the principle reflected in paragraph 2(c) of § 317. Fred McGriff had negotiated for the right to have a no-trade provision in his contract. The Devil Rays were therefore precluded from trading him, a fact which necessitated McGriff's waiver before the Cubs could acquire him.

---

## Source

"After Balking, McGriff Blows Into Chicago; Five-Time All-Star's Trade Gives the Cubs Extra Punch, Protection for Sosa," *The Washington Post*, 28 July 2001, D7.

## References

RESTATEMENT (SECOND) OF CONTRACTS §§ 317, 318, 322 (1981).

### § 317. Assignment of a Right

(1) An assignment of a right is a manifestation of the assignor's intention to transfer it by virtue of which the assignor's right to performance by the obligor is extinguished in whole or in part and the assignee acquires a right to such performance.

(2) A contractual right can be assigned unless:

    (a) the substitution of a right of the assignee for the right of the assignor would materially change the duty of the obligor, or materially increase the burden or risk imposed on him by his contract, or materially impair his chance of obtaining return performance, or materially reduce its value to him, or

    (b) the assignment is forbidden by statute or is otherwise inoperative on grounds of public policy, or

    (c) assignment is validly precluded by contract.

### § 318. Delegation of Performance of Duty

(1) An obligor can properly delegate the performance of his duty to another unless the delegation is contrary to public policy or the terms of his promise.

(2) Unless otherwise agreed, a promise requires performance by a particular person only to the extent that the obligee has a substantial interest in having that person perform or control the acts promised.

(3) Unless the obligee agrees otherwise, neither delegation of performance nor a contract to assume the duty made with the obligor by the person delegated discharges any duty or liability of the delegating obligor.

## § 322. Contractual Prohibition of Assignment

(1) Unless the circumstances indicate the contrary, a contract term prohibiting assignment of "the contract" bars only the delegation to an assignee of the performance by the assignor of a duty or condition.

(2) A contract term prohibiting assignment of rights under the contract, unless a different intention is manifested,

    (a) does not forbid assignment of a right to damages for breach of the whole contract or a right arising out of the assignor's due performance of his entire obligation;

    (b) gives the obligor a right to damages for breach of the terms forbidding assignment but does not render the assignment ineffective;

    (c) is for the benefit of the obligor, and does not prevent the assignee from acquiring rights against the assignor or the obligor from discharging his duty as if there were no such prohibition.

# Trading the Wizard

## Situation

Ozzie "The Wizard" Smith began his major league baseball career with the San Diego Padres in 1978. For four years, Smith wielded his magic at shortstop for the Padres. Throughout his time with the Padres, Smith fielded his position with unparalleled flair but failed to show prowess as a hitter. In 1981, he hit only .222, prompting the Padres to look for other options at shortstop. In December 1981, the Padres told Smith that they were going to trade him to the St. Louis Cardinals as part of a multi-player deal. In exchange, the Padres would receive Cardinals shortstop Garry Templeton, a lifetime .304 hitter. At the time, Smith's contract with the Padres included a no-trade clause. The Padres did not seek a waiver from Smith before negotiating the trade. As Smith tells the story, he was left to wonder what had happened to his no-trade clause.

## Issue

Were the San Diego Padres liable to Smith for breach of contract in failing to honor the no-trade clause in his contract?

## Analysis

The principle articulated in § 317 of the Restatement of Contracts enables teams to assign a player's contract to another team unless the assignment is precluded by contract. The Padres were validly precluded by contract from trading Ozzie Smith. Seeking to acquire a hitter of Templeton's stature and perhaps unmindful of Smith's no-trade clause, the Padres worked out the deal with the Cardinals. Under Section § 322 of the Restatement of Contracts, Smith (the "obligor") would have been entitled to seek compensation for damages from the Padres for breach of contract, but the assignment of his player contract to the Cardinals would remain effective.

In fact, after learning of the trade, Smith balked at relocating to St. Louis. Believing that his team would be a bona fide contender for the National League crown with "The Wizard" at shortstop, St. Louis manager Whitey Herzog set out to convince Smith to agree to the trade. Herzog ultimately wore down Smith's resistance. In February 1982, Smith agreed to waive his no-trade clause and the deal was completed. Herzog proved prophetic, as the Cardinals advanced to the 1982 World Series with Smith at shortstop. St. Louis defeated the Milwaukee Brewers in the Series, four games to three.

## Source

"Cardinals Complete Deal for Ozzie Smith," *The Washington Post*, 12 February 1982, D3.

## References

RESTATEMENT (SECOND) OF CONTRACTS §§ 317, 318, 322 (1981).

### § 317. Assignment of a Right

(1) An assignment of a right is a manifestation of the assignor's intention to transfer it by virtue of which the assignor's right to performance by the obligor is extinguished in whole or in part and the assignee acquires a right to such performance.

(2) A contractual right can be assigned unless:

(a) the substitution of a right of the assignee for the right of the assignor would materially change the duty of the obligor, or materially increase the burden or risk imposed on him by his contract, or materially impair his chance of obtaining return performance, or materially reduce its value to him, or

(b) the assignment is forbidden by statute or is otherwise inoperative on grounds of public policy, or

(c) assignment is validly precluded by contract.

### § 318. Delegation of Performance of Duty

(1) An obligor can properly delegate the performance of his duty to another unless the delegation is contrary to public policy or the terms of his promise.

(2) Unless otherwise agreed, a promise requires performance by a particular person only to the extent that the obligee has a substantial interest in having that person perform or control the acts promised.

(3) Unless the obligee agrees otherwise, neither delegation of performance nor a contract to assume the duty made with the obligor by the person delegated discharges any duty or liability of the delegating obligor.

### § 322. Contractual Prohibition of Assignment

(1) Unless the circumstances indicate the contrary, a contract term prohibiting assignment of "the contract" bars only the delegation to an assignee of the performance by the assignor of a duty or condition.

(2) A contract term prohibiting assignment of rights under the contract, unless a different intention is manifested,

    (a) does not forbid assignment of a right to damages for breach of the whole contract or a right arising out of the assignor's due performance of his entire obligation;

    (b) gives the obligor a right to damages for breach of the terms forbidding assignment but does not render the assignment ineffective;

    (c) is for the benefit of the obligor, and does not prevent the assignee from acquiring rights against the assignor or the obligor from discharging his duty as if there were no such prohibition.

# Same Team, Different Owner

## Situation

In the late 1960s, Los Angeles Rams quarterback Roman Gabriel was one of the marquee players in the NFL. A collegiate standout at North Carolina State, Gabriel was the National Football League's Most Valuable Player in 1969. Gabriel asked for, and received, a "no-trade" provision in his contract with the Rams. The provision prohibited the Rams from selling, exchanging, assigning or transferring Gabriel's player contract to any other team in the National Football League. In 1973, Gabriel's stature suffered when the Rams acquired fellow quarterback John Hadl from the San Diego Chargers. Gabriel did not welcome the prospect of sharing playing time with Hadl and wanted out of Los Angeles. Coincidentally, the ownership of the Rams had changed hands the previous year. The new owner, Carroll Rosenbloom, acquired the team after Gabriel had signed his contract with the Rams. Seeking to force a trade, Gabriel claimed that the previous owners of the Rams had violated the no-trade clause in his contract when they sold the team to Rosenbloom. Gabriel's lawyer explained, "Gabriel has an agreement in writing with a company no longer in existence, and without his approval, his contract could not be assigned." Gabriel sued the Rams and asked for $5,000 in damages for violation of his contract.

## Issue

Did the sale of the Rams to Carroll Rosenbloom violate the no-trade clause in Roman Gabriel's contract?

## Analysis

Section 280 of the Restatement of Contracts defines a "novation" as a substituted contract that includes as a party one who was not a party to the original contract. Gabriel and his lawyer were attempting to depict the change in ownership as the equivalent of a novation. Clearly, a novation would have been inconsistent with Gabriel's no-trade clause. When news of Gabriel's ploy became public, Gabriel's lawyer acknowledged that the tactic might not work. "This hasn't been tried before, but he's got nothing to lose," the lawyer said. "If he loses, he'll be right back where he is now."

The legal grounds underlying Gabriel's position were suspect. Though the owner had changed, the team remained the same. Seeking to resolve the issue, the Rams ultimately agreed to trade Gabriel to the Philadelphia Eagles. Shortly before the teams finalized the trade, Gabriel withdrew his lawsuit.

## Sources

"Gabriel Files Suit Disputing Ram Contract," *The Washington Post*, 10 May 1973, D4.

"Gabriel Suit Dismissed," *The Washington Post*, 31 May 1973, D5.

## References

RESTATEMENT (SECOND) OF CONTRACTS §§ 280, 322 (1981).

### § 280. Novation

A novation is a substituted contract that includes as a party one who was neither the obligor nor the obligee of the original duty.

### § 322. Contractual Prohibition of Assignment

(1) Unless the circumstances indicate the contrary, a contract term prohibiting assignment of "the contract" bars only the delegation to an assignee of the performance by the assignor of a duty or condition.

(2) A contract term prohibiting assignment of rights under the contract, unless a different intention is manifested,

(a) does not forbid assignment of a right to damages for breach of the whole contract or a right arising out of the assignor's due performance of his entire obligation;

(b) gives the obligor a right to damages for breach of the terms forbidding assignment but does not render the assignment ineffective;

(c) is for the benefit of the obligor, and does not prevent the assignee from acquiring rights against the assignor or the obligor from discharging his duty as if there were no such prohibition.

# The Law of Free Agency

## Situation

In the spring of 1975, pitcher John Alexander "Andy" Messersmith was unable to reach agreement with the Los Angeles Dodgers on what he considered to be a fair salary for the upcoming season. In 1974, Messersmith had started 39 games for the Dodgers and won 20 of them, with 13 complete games. Along the way, he pitched three shutouts, lost only six games and gave up only 2.59 runs every nine innings. His performance propelled the Dodgers to the World Series. Messersmith was seeking a substantial raise for 1975. The Dodgers balked.

As was standard for all major league player contracts at the time, there was a team option clause in Messersmith's 1974 contract. The option clause gave the Dodgers the right "to renew this contract for the period of one year on the same terms." When Messersmith refused to sign a contract for the 1975 season, the Dodgers exercised their option and unilaterally renewed his contract at a modest increase in salary.

Following the 1975 season, Messersmith filed a grievance under baseball's Collective Bargaining Agreement. Messersmith sought to be declared a free agent. He argued that the Dodgers were entitled to unilaterally renew his contract for one year only. Since he had not signed a contract for 1975, Messersmith argued he was no longer subject to the option clause. In response, the Dodgers insisted that they continued to hold the rights to Messersmith for 1976. The Dodgers maintained that, when they unilaterally renewed a player's contract, they also bought themselves an option on the player's services for the following year. In the Dodgers' view, the option provision allowed a team to renew a player's contract year after year.

## Issue

Did the Los Angeles Dodgers gain an option for Messersmith's services during the 1976 season by virtue of having unilaterally renewed his contract for 1975?

## Analysis

Under § 235 of the Restatement of Contracts, full performance of a duty under a contract discharges the duty. Section 235 suggests that, when Messersmith threw his last pitch of the 1975 season for the Dodgers, he had fulfilled his legal duty to the team under the terms of the contract that the Dodgers had unilaterally renewed.

Having given the Dodgers the one year, 1975, to which they were entitled under his previous contract, Messersmith believed that he was a free agent in 1976 and able to sign with any team. As required by baseball's Collective Bargaining Agreement, the dispute was referred to an arbitrator. The arbitrator, Peter Seitz, examined major league baseball rules, the Collective Bargaining Agreement, and the standard player contract. In particular, Seitz reviewed the wording in the option clause in Messersmith's contract for 1974. Seitz ruled that the option clause extended for one year only and not perpetually, as the Dodgers insisted. In a decision issued in December 1975, Seitz held that major league teams could not legally reserve the services of players, such as Messersmith, who were no longer under contract. Seitz declared Messersmith to be a free agent and therefore able to sign with any other team.

---

## Source

Roger I. Abrams, *Legal Bases: Baseball and the Law* (Philadelphia, PA: Temple University Press, 1998), 127.

## References

RESTATEMENT (SECOND) OF CONTRACTS §§ 25, 223, 235 (1981).

### § 25. Option Contracts

An option contract is a promise which meets the requirements for the formation of a contract and limits the promisor's power to revoke an offer.

### § 223. Course of Dealing

(1) A course of dealing is a sequence of previous conduct between the parties to an agreement which is fairly to be regarded as establishing a common basis of understanding for interpreting their expressions and other conduct.

(2) Unless otherwise agreed, a course of dealing between the parties gives meaning to or supplements or qualifies their agreement.

### § 235. Effect of Performance as Discharge and of Non-Performance as Breach

(1) Full performance of a duty under a contract discharges the duty.

(2) When performance of a duty under a contract is due any non-performance is a breach.

# *Destroying the Legal Relationship*

## Down the Toilet

### Situation

In the 1960s and 1970s, teams from the National Basketball Association and the rival American Basketball Association competed to sign the top college players. After 6'11" Bob McAdoo completed his career at the University of North Carolina, the ABA's Virginia Squires signed him to a contract. McAdoo had completed his college eligibility but was still enrolled in school. The Squires had reason to think that the contract might not stand up in court, because McAdoo was under twenty-one when he signed. Out of caution, the Squires decided to keep the contract secret and store it in a safety-deposit box. The contract became of concern when the NBA's Buffalo Braves drafted McAdoo. Braves owner Paul Snyder got wind of McAdoo's ABA contract and called the Squires. The Braves wanted McAdoo badly. Snyder offered Earl Foreman, owner of the Squires, $200,000 to forego the rights to McAdoo. Foreman, thinking that the contract with McAdoo was unenforceable to begin with, was stunned. He quickly accepted Snyder's offer. Together, the rival owners went to Foreman's safety-deposit box and retrieved the contract. With the contract finally in his hands, Snyder wanted to make sure that the Squires would never try to assert any rights to McAdoo. Snyder lit the contract with a match, dropped it into a toilet bowl, and flushed.

### Issue

Was Paul Snyder's act sufficient to destroy the legal relationship between the Virginia Squires and Bob McAdoo?

### Analysis

Section 71 of the Restatement of Contracts describes the various actions that may form the consideration for a binding contract. Under § 71(3)(c), an agreement to destroy a legal relationship is valid consideration. There is no doubt that the Virginia Squires provided valid consideration for the bargain with the Buffalo Braves. For purposes of demonstrating that Bob McAdoo's legal relationship with the Virginia Squires was over, could there be any more convincing form of destruction than to flush the contract down the toilet?

As reflected in § 274 of the Restatement, a duty under a formal contract is integrally related to the writing that embodies it. The law holds that the legal relationship will not survive the document's destruction, if that act is done by the obligee with the intention of discharging the duty. When Earl Foreman surrendered the contract to Paul Snyder and permitted Snyder to flush it down the toilet, it eliminated any possibility that the Virginia Squires might assert the legal right to McAdoo's talents.

## Source

Terry Pluto, *Loose Balls: The Short, Wild Life of the American Basketball Association As Told by the Players, Coaches, and Movers and Shakers Who Made It Happen* (New York: Simon and Schuster, 1990), 196.

## References

RESTATEMENT (SECOND) OF CONTRACTS §§ 71, 274 (1981).

### § 71. Requirement of Exchange; Types of Exchange

(1) To constitute consideration, a performance or a return promise must be bargained for.

(2) A performance or return promise is bargained for if it is sought by the promisor in exchange for his promise and is given by the promisee in exchange for that promise.

(3) The performance may consist of

   (a) an act other than a promise, or

   (b) a forbearance, or

   (c) the creation, modification, or destruction of a legal relation.

(4) The performance or return promise may be given to the promisor or to some other person. It may be given by the promisee or by some other person.

### § 274. Cancellation, Destruction, or Surrender of a Writing

An obligee's cancellation, destruction or surrender to the obligor of a writing of a type customarily accepted as a symbol or as evidence of his right discharges without consideration the obligor's duty if it is done with the manifested intention to discharge it.

# Conclusion

In January 2005, Fred Chamberlain, an Orlando, Florida maintenance engineer, sued Houston Rockets all-star shooting guard Tracy McGrady for injuries inflicted by McGrady's pet Rottweiler, Max. On August 24, 2004, Chamberlain was working at McGrady's mansion in Orlando when Max attacked him, biting off the tip of Chamberlain's nose. ("McGrady Is Sued for Dog Attack," *The Washington Post*, 21 January 2005, D1.)

There was no question as to the cause of Chamberlain's injury. "It was my dog, and it damn near bit somebody's nose off," McGrady conceded. McGrady was quick to add that Max, though usually nice, could be "very vicious." There was, however, an element of intrigue underlying the attack. News reports indicated that Max was trained to attack on command. Chamberlain's lawyer suggested that perhaps someone in the house had instructed Max to attack Chamberlain.

The revelation that Max was trained to attack on command brought with it significant legal implications. If McGrady had simply failed to exercise proper control over Max, he would have been liable for negligently exposing Chamberlain to an unreasonable risk of harm, an unintentional tort. On the other hand, if someone in McGrady's household had actually instructed Max to attack Chamberlain, the act would constitute willful misconduct and an **intentional tort**.

The distinction is important. If Max's attack was found to be the result of negligence, McGrady would likely be permitted to raise, in his defense, evidence of **contributory negligence**, if any, by Chamberlain. If Max's attack was found to be the result of an intentional tort, McGrady would not be permitted to rely on contributory negligence in his defense. The distinction between negligence and intentional tort could also affect whether McGrady's home owner insurance policy would cover any damages that might be awarded to Chamberlain.

In earlier era, the discussion of whether McGrady or members of his household might be liable for an intentional tort would have been confined largely to law school classes. Those days have passed. In the current era, what happens within the walls of McGrady's house will be discussed and debated in the lunch rooms

205

and meeting rooms across America and on radio talk shows—especially when the topic is as tantalizing as an attack by a "very vicious" Rottweiler. Now more than ever, sports commentators and their listeners are as quick to offer comment on the likely outcome of trials involving prominent athletes as on the advantages and liabilities of the **West Coast Offense.**

When compiling the Restatements of Contracts and Torts, the drafters had no inkling that "no-trade" clauses would become commonplace in professional sports, or that a roster bonus might one day be priced at $6.5 million. They had no inkling that women would someday compete for jobs as major league umpires. In short, the drafters would have been hard-pressed to predict the dramatic changes that have occurred in sports and in society in the decades since the Restatements were published.

Nonetheless, the principles of law reflected in the Restatements are sufficiently versatile to provide meaningful guidance in today's world of sports. The Restatements allow us to sort out the contractual obligations when a Fred McGriff seeks to enforce his no-trade clause. They speak with clarity on an issue such as LaVar Arrington's assertion that the Washington Redskins owe him a $6.5 million bonus. They provide a basis for rendering judgment when a baseball manager threatens to kiss a woman umpire on the playing field. And, in the case of injuries inflicted by a vicious Rottweiler, they provide a basis for distinguishing between simple negligence and an intentional tort.

Some twenty-five years after publication, the Restatements continue to offer a ready means of analysis for even the most complex legal problems that arise in the world of sports and elsewhere.

# About the Author

Fred Day is a lawyer and inveterate sports fan. He holds a master's degree in political economics from the State University of New York (Albany) and a law degree from George Washington University. His previous book on sports and the law, *Clubhouse Lawyer: Law in the World of Sports*, was proclaimed "a jewel" by the Blue Ridge Business Journal. He has written a series of articles on sports and the law for the *Fairfax (Virginia) Bar Journal* and is a frequent guest on sports-talk radio programs throughout the country. He has also published three books on the Federal Communications Commission and wireless telecommunications systems. Day maintains a law practice in Falls Church, Virginia.

0-595-34315-5

Printed in the United States
111176LV00007B/172/A